Death
by
Theory

D1408859

A TALE OF MYSTERY AND ARCHAEOLOGICAL THEORY

Adrian Praetzellis

ALTAMIRA
PRESS

A Division of
ROWMAN & LITTLEFIELD PUBLISHERS, INC.
Lanham • New York • Toronto • Oxford

ALTAMIRA PRESS
A division of Rowman & Littlefield Publishers, Inc.
4501 Forbes Boulevard, Suite 200
Lanham, MD 20706

PO Box 317
Oxford
OX2 9RU, UK

Copyright © 2000 by AltaMira Press

All rights reserved. No part of this publication may be reproduced,
stored in a retrieval system, or transmitted in any form or by any
means, electronic, mechanical, photocopying, recording, or otherwise,
without the prior permission of the publisher.

British Library Cataloguing-in-Publication Information Available

Library of Congress Cataloging-in-Publication Data

Praetzellis, Adrian, 1952–
    Death by theory : a tale of mystery and archaeological theory / Adrian Praetzellis.
      p. cm.
    Includes bibliographical references and index.
    ISBN   978-0-7425-0359-5 —ISBN 0-7425-0359-3 (paper : alk.
paper)
      1. Archaeology.   2. Archaeology—Methodology.   I. Title.

    CC72.P73   2000
    930.1'01—dc21   00-057601

Printed in the United States of America

♾ ™ The paper used in this publication meets the minimum requirements of
American National Standard for Information Sciences—Permanence of Paper for
Printed Library Materials, ANSI/NISO Z39.48–1992.

Contents

Acknowledgments

This wouldn't have been possible without Mary, who gave me the freedom to play writer. Mitch Allen still doesn't know if this whole mystery/theory thing will turn out to be an awful mistake or the beginning of his new life of ease. (We're both hoping for the latter.) Penny Warner laughed at the funny bits and told me not to give up. The anonymous reviewers (they know who they are, though I don't) were kind enough to spend their time looking over the manuscript and making pages of helpful suggestions. Of course, none of these worthy scholars is responsible for errors of fact or interpretation that they may have overlooked; that's all my doing.

"A" IS FOR ARCHAEOLOGY

In Which Dr. Green and Mr. Doyle Are Enlisted

With massive breasts and great globe-like ass, the image flickering on the screen was a vision of fecund sensuality. An object of erotic desire, even religious devotion, he supposed.

Sean Doyle stifled a yawn and considered whether or not he could discreetly bail on the performance. As a rule, he wasn't immune to feminine charms. It was just that this particular woman was three inches high and several thousand years old. Neolithic archaeology had never held much interest for Sean; too many rocks and no written sources to temper what seemed to him to be the overactive archaeological imagination.

In fact, this entire trip to the Society for American Archeology's annual meeting was turning out to be something of a dud. The only morning session he had marked with a check on his conference program—a series of papers on cemetery archaeology—had been filled to overflowing by writers of midlist mystery novels whose protagonists were spunky forensic anthropologists with idiosyncratic pets and names like Kate and Kinsey. Sean had been forced to sit outside in the hall and contemplate the inequity of the conference's $110 registration fee.

The speaker droned on, interrupted only by her sneezing fits. More slides of enormously endowed figurines. Sean tapped his companion's shoulder and whispered so close to her ear that his cheek brushed one of her gray curls and he smelled the patchouli.

"Do you want to get outta here?" he hissed. "I can't stand any more of 'The World According to Marija Gimbutas.'"

"Not a fan of ecofeminist archaeology, Sean?" she goaded. "OK, I'm sort of starting to snooze myself. But let's be unobtrusive because the speaker's a friend of mine."

They got up and shuffled as quietly as they could along the row of chairs to the side aisle.

"I can see its appeal, though," he continued when they were out of the meeting room. "You know—the idea that the Neolithic in southeastern Europe was a peaceful, egalitarian . . ."

". . . matriarchal, goddess-worshipping era. Yes, it has a certain appeal to me, too. But, well . . ." His colleague paused with a lopsided half smile.

"Yeah, I know what you're going to say, *Doctor* Green: there's just not much evidence that it ever happened."

Hannah Green noted the cynical edge to her nephew's voice and knew that she had been too free with her own critiques. *The problem in hanging out with cynical old hag-archaeologists like you*, she told herself, *is that at this point, Sean doesn't believe anything an archaeologist says that isn't a matter of empirical fact. My fault. Damn it.*

"But it's a nice, optimistic story all the same," she said with a grin, resolving henceforth to be less critical in his hearing.

The two sat side by side on the vinyl-covered bench, their backs against the wall, vaguely watching the conference-goers bustle past. They made an unremarkable couple, the young man and his archaeologist aunt, and most who bothered to spare them a glance took the pair as student and professor: Sean Doyle looked younger than his twenty-three years and hardly even resented being carded at bars anymore. Blond-haired—well not exactly blond, more that mousy brown that turns light in the summer and darkens up by January—and good looking in a high-school jock sort of a way, he was inclined to be taciturn, a trait, or so his aunt believed, derived from the boy's childhood in the upper Midwest and an Episcopalian father. But the casual observer who guessed "undergrad" got it wrong. With a six-month-old anthropology B.A. in his pocket, Sean was out in the world and scouting around for whatever might turn up in the way of a career. And graduate school in archaeology seemed like a good enough way to put off the decision for another few years.

"Listen, boychik, grad school is a big step," his aunt declared with much finger wagging at his graduation party. Sean had always been a great romantic, dropping everything for the sake of each new obsession. "Take my advice," said Hannah, "and go find out what archaeology is about before you commit to it. Spend a year with a government agency or, even better, a contract archaeology firm. Learn how archaeology is really done, then decide if it's what you want to do."

It had seemed like good advice. And besides, his mother refused to come up with any money for tuition unless he followed her sister's suggestion. The latter consideration had settled it, and Sean spent eight months out of the last twelve working as a grunt for archaeological consultants between Illinois and Missouri, digging square holes and tramping through blackberry bushes allegedly for the purpose of archaeological survey. Now it was May, and he was out of work and attending the association meetings for the sole purpose of scoping out the employment possibilities. His aunt was hardly one of the big shots in North American archaeology, but she should have a few contacts. Or so it was to be hoped. Sean's fantasy was to work his way west and south as an itinerant archaeologist. California would be nice; dig during the day, then down to the beach for a happening social life. But all he'd been offered was a place on a pipeline survey in Oklahoma.

"It's a nice story, huh?" quizzed Sean. "Is that all archaeology is— just a bunch of stories? Don't archaeologists think of themselves as scientists anymore? Testing theories and that sort of thing?"

Right now, Sean was more concerned with whether or not they had blackberry bushes in Oklahoma, and if eight dollars an hour for schlepping dirt was likely to go farther there than it did in Illinois.

"And just *how many* units did *you* take in archaeology?" Hannah regretted her sarcasm as soon as the words were out of her mouth. Her ability to give emphasis to words as if she were saying them in capital letters was a useful trait in a university lecturer, but, as she was aware, some found it rather trying in an informal conversation.

"Listen, boychik," she began, trying for a lighter tone, "scientists, even archaeologists, don't test theories. They test *hypotheses*." The

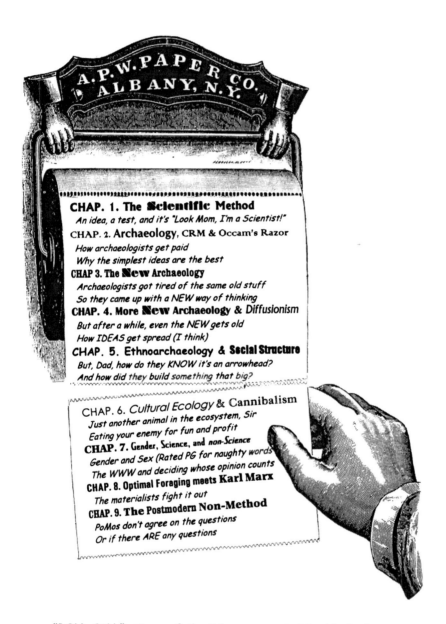

"ROLL CALL": Some of the Ideas presented in this Book

blank look on her nephew's face showed that the distinction was not clear, so she continued in what she hoped was not an overly teachy manner.

"Stop me if you've heard this one, but science is nothing more than a way of organizing what you know about a subject so that you can understand it better. If you're going to use the scientific method, you have to put all your assumptions on the table, be explicit about the relationship between what you want to know and your method for finding it out, and be willing to be wrong. The scientific method involves starting out with an idea about why something is the way it is—a theory. Then you come up with a number of plausible explanations or hypotheses that you can apply to the facts of the case to see which fit and which don't."

Sean frowned. "But everyone's entitled to their own opinion, aren't they?"

"Sure. And part of the point of using the scientific method is to separate opinion—which can be based on faulty information, poor reasoning, or just plain old personal bias—from ideas that can be verified. People have hopelessly ill-informed opinions about all manner of topics. The scientific method comes up with a conclusion you trust because you can follow the reasoning that leads up to it. Opinion is cheap. Scientific rigor is something else."

"OK, but you're really begging the question. Is archaeology a science or isn't it?"

"Perhaps I'm not answering because I don't like your question." Hannah turned some of the bracelets on her skinny left wrist. "This science or not-a-science business is a bit of a false dichotomy. Archaeology isn't a science in the same way that chemistry is. Listen. The scientific method works best when people can test their ideas by making predictions and seeing if things turn out the way they expect. A chemist can mix up a batch of chemicals under the same conditions several days in a row and confidently predict that she will have the same end product every time. Archaeologists can make *some* predictive statements—that you will find sites next to water or even that the ability to create an agricultural surplus goes hand in hand with social complexity. But people aren't as predictable as chemicals, and they don't follow universal laws of behavior that we

ARE ALL FISH BLUE FISH?

Using the SCIENTIFIC approach we begin with an IDEA, test it using systematically collected DATA, and REVISE the idea if necessary. Conversely, if we HAPHAZARDLY pull data out of the Sea of Facts there's no way of knowing if what we catch is REPRESENTATIVE of what's actually out there or if it's just a product of HOW we did our collecting.

can use to predict—or should I say retro-dict—what they did in the past."

Sean stifled a yawn. He shouldn't have started her going.

"There are plenty who would disagree," continued Hannah enthusiastically. "But if you ask me, science is only a means to a more important end. As an archaeologist, I use tools, like the scientific method, to approach questions that are essentially humanistic, that is, to learn about people in the past as entities that had real humanity and weren't just puppets whose strings were pulled by a supposedly immutable law of behavior, by the environment, or some other uncontrollable force."

Sean considered this for a few moments and found himself fairly satisfied. Or at least out-intellectualized.

"All right, Dr. Science, but who comes up with the idea, the theory, in the first place? Is *that* part of the scientific method?"

"Not at all. There's no big book of archaeological research questions that only Ph.D.s are allowed to peer into at midnight on the full moon. It doesn't matter much *where* the original idea comes from so long as it's interesting and you can actually get at it using archaeological data. In reality, research questions often come from a combination of the archaeologist's own interests and what people are writing about in the professional journals and talking about at conferences like this." Hannah gestured toward a clutch of tweed jackets who were busy nodding and gesticulating to each other over by the coffee stand.

"So it's just a matter of fashion?" said Sean. "Don't archaeologists ever find out the truth? This year the environment explains everything, but next year everyone is looking at genes for the big answer. Is that it?"

"Now let's not be glib, Sean. And don't forget the immortal words of that great, if fictional, archaeologist Indiana Jones: 'If you want the Truth, try the Philosophy Department.'"

As he was wont to do when a conversation turned what he considered overly high-brow, Sean rolled his eyes. "And just what does that mean?"

"Only that archaeologists don't claim to have the *one and only answer*. In fact, most often we don't come up with what most people

would call an answer at all. For most of us, it's enough to contribute
to the *understanding* of an issue without believing that we have to
arrive at the ultimate cause behind some historical event or social
process to justify our research. But to get back to questions, often
they come out of some peculiarity in your data that you want to
explain."

"Such as?"

Hannah fiddled some more with her bracelets, causing them to
jingle softly. She needed a good example; simple but clear. Over by
the coffee pot, a young man with an acne-afflicted face and a middle-
aged woman, both in regulation black aprons, were refilling the
matching wicker bowls with little packets; white for sugar, pink for
Sweet 'n Low.

"Remember when you and your mom visited that site I was digging over by Markleyville?" It had been two years since Hannah directed the field school on that Midwestern site and she hoped that her
nephew recalled the place. At the time, he had been more interested
in studying the after-hours social life of archaeologists in the field
than in their daytime doings.

The nephew smiled slyly. "I remember thinking that archaeologists
are big on parties."

"Which I'm sure had no influence on your choice of career,"
replied the aunt in mock disapproval. "So, as you remember, the site
had been partly excavated the year before by Ian . . . well, by another
archaeologist, as our department's summer archaeological field
school. He, this other archaeologist, had excavated several of these
bowl-shaped depressions and found that each one was surrounded by
a series of postholes, indicating that they had been buildings with
walls and a roof. And a couple of feet under the floor in the center of
each, they'd found a human skeleton, formally buried with grave
goods and all. Since there were almost no artifacts on the surface inside the little buildings, my colleague concluded that the buildings
were burial chambers. Tombs."

"Sounds like a reasonable conclusion to me."

"Except that they looked *exactly* like what the local Native Americans were calling pit-houses—simple huts whose floors are dug into
the ground."

Sean shrugged and thumbed through his conference program. "Perhaps they were wrong."

"Perhaps. But there are many peoples who bury their dead in their houses and then abandon them or burn them down. So why couldn't that have happened here? To find out for sure I put together a simple hypothesis. I reasoned that if they *were* houses, we could explain the absence of artifacts inside if they were regularly swept out. If the hypothesis was right, I predicted that we would find the domestic artifacts, the peoples' daily trash, adjacent to the building's doorway. To test the hypothesis, we excavated a broad area of the ground's surface outside each building." She paused for dramatic effect.

He looked up from the program. "And?"

"And, as a matter of fact, we found what we expected. The ancient ground surface was littered with potsherds, fragments of food bones, and other good stuff. So my hypothesis survived the test. You see, by focusing on the most dramatic remains, the other archaeologist missed the most interpretively useful part of the site. He went for the flash and ignored the substance."

Although to be fair, she conceded to herself, the blame could be spread around, for their department chairman wasn't interested in spending precious funds on a discovery that amounted to a scatter of pottery and a few bits of old bone. That wouldn't attract more students to the department's chronically underenrolled field school.

Nor, incidentally, did the discovery help Hannah to get a tenured position on the anthropology department faculty at Ennui State University when she came up for review the following spring. Undermining the professional reputation of one of your colleagues isn't considered the most effective strategy by which to gain his support. At the time of the vote, said colleague called in a favor, and Hannah's bid for job security had to wait for another year.

That was her problem, she scolded herself. Too direct and combative. Too sure of herself, even when she was wrong. It was a piece of Israeli culture, like her contempt for waiting in lines, that had become part of her makeup in the five years that she spent in the country.

Hannah Green had made her *aliyah* (going up) to Israel at the age of twenty-two, and had soon found a job as an archaeological monitor with the national antiquities department. While many North

Americans think of preserving the evidence of their country's history as a pastime for the overeducated and underemployed, in Israel, archaeology and national identity are inextricably bound—and nationhood is, quite literally, a matter of life and death. And so it came to be that after two years of glorious freedom roving the country in a Jeep, Hannah found herself drafted into the army as a member of an occupation "essential to national security." In public, she admitted to being in the Education Corps. For the few in the know, this translated to furtive, nighttime excursions into no-go portions of the West Bank and Sinai to check on the veracity of rumored discoveries by Jordanian and Egyptian archaeologists that periodically set the country buzzing. After her army service and a short but ultimately bitter romantic interlude that nixed her chances for graduate school in Israel, Hannah wangled a place at London's Institute of Archaeology studying the origins of agriculture in prehistoric western Europe. It was a long way from the Golan Heights to Ennui State University, but Hannah soon discovered that while politics are not pursued with such deadly force on campus as in the Near East, it isn't for lack of conviction.

Sean dropped his program and it slid under the bench. "Well, OK," he conceded grudgingly. "I suppose it makes sense. But that was a pretty simple hypothesis. How about the big ideas that supposedly make sense of everything. Everyone knows that archaeology can help us to date sites and to reconstruct how people lived in the past. But all those 'isms' and 'ists' that I had to memorize for my History of Archaeology final? I never could see how they really help anyone to understand archaeology."

"And which 'isms' did you have in mind?" inquired Hannah over her steel rimmed glasses. OK, so she needed bifocals. But she'd be damned if she'd get them.

"Oh, Marxism, cultural materialism, neoevolutionism, functionalism, postmodernism," he rattled off the names in rapid succession. "The stuff that you're writing about in your book."

Hannah winced. The draft of her undergraduate textbook, *Archaeology from A to Z*, was a long way from being complete, and she was working on her second time extension. Using Sue Grafton's successful alphabet murder series to structure an archaeological textbook had seemed like a good idea at the time, but the problem was making one theme build on the next. Of course, it was just a gimmick. But the question remained whether or not it was a gimmick that would work. She had no money to pay a real illustrator and her hard-hearted editor had insisted that authors pay the costs to use other published graphics. Consequently, Hannah was reduced to using her own artwork—a peculiar convergence of cartooning and Monty Python-like montage—to illustrate her words. Would Lascaux Press be amused? Who could say? The editor had warned her that a draft was due by September, or else. There was no need to complete the threat, for it is well known in the halls of academe that would-be authors of archaeology texts are two a penny and publishers jettison the flaky ones like yesterday's underwear.

"How about this," offered Hannah, seeking to temper Sean's empiricist bent, "if you give me the chance to show you how having a theoretical perspective is a useful way of understanding what happened in the past, I'll see what I can do about getting you employed for the summer."

He shrugged. "Why not? Nothing to lose."

So deeply had our protagonists submerged themselves in anthropological musings that neither noticed the figure who discreetly joined them. He stood halfway turned toward the conversationalists, his head cocked to take it all in. Dr. Ian Tuliver was a shortish man whose entry into early middle age had been marked by an incipient heaviness around the waist, attended by thinning hair, which he swept directly back over his crown. The boyish visage, which in his early career engendered certain extrascholastic yearnings on the part of more than one female graduate student, had developed a distinct double chin, giving him the appearance of a debauched schoolboy.

"Doing a little after-class instruction?" inquired Tuliver. The shallowly concealed innuendo belied his open smile.

Hannah sighed at the unwelcome sound of her colleague's whine. Annoyed by the interruption, she acknowledged his presence by rising regally from her vinyl throne. At a shade under six feet, she had an advantage of four inches over Tuliver, causing him to back off a couple of steps into a concrete column. The munificent smile, however, remained fixed on his chubby face.

"Am I to take it that your young *friend* is looking for work on an excavation?"

Oblivious to the suggestive intonation that Tuliver had attached to the word, Sean perked up and offered the haughty academic his hand.

"Because if he is," continued Tuliver, grasping the young man's hand with both of his own pink paws in a fair impersonation of a car dealer moving in for a sale, "if he is, I may have something for him."

Grinning and nodding like the village idiot, Sean assured the professor that he was most interested indeed. Oddly, Tuliver seemed to be more concerned with his colleague's reaction than Sean's. A tight feeling in her throat told Hannah that there was more to Tuliver's solicitousness than a desire to advance the career of a young man whom he had just met.

Yet, Tuliver was strangely reticent when she asked about the site: Where was it? What was it? To these and to other mundane questions, the man would only smile and say it was an exciting and potentially controversial site, and that all would be revealed if the pair would meet him later. Reluctantly, Hannah agreed—what else could she do with Sean bouncing around like a large puppy on the verge of a romp in the park? The time was set, more damp handshakes were exchanged, and Tuliver insinuated himself back into the sea of herringbone tweed and respectably faded Levi's.

★ ★ ★ ★

One overpriced dinner later, the elder of our pair of not particularly well-fed archaeologists pushed the button for the fourteenth floor of the hotel. Their distorted images stared back at them from the elevator's reflective, faux brass walls on which Sean nervously drummed his fingers, creating small oily patches. The only other passenger, an elderly woman whose eyes did not leave her shoes, got out on the thirteenth. As the doors closed, she turned and nodded at Hannah, touching the brim of her straw hat in acknowledgment. Sean turned to grin at his aunt, who forced a smile in return.

Before dinner, Hannah had taken off the heavy Southwestern-style necklace and changed into a severe, loose-fitting black dress and boots that added at least two inches to her already considerable stature.

Tuliver could be as slippery and manipulative as a politician. But whatever the *mamser* was up to, he would find Hannah Green ready for action and all business.

Room 1434 was near the end of a long, carpeted corridor, next to the soft drink machine. The door was ajar but Hannah carefully knocked on the jamb. She did not want to cause it to swing open, having absolutely no desire to catch her colleague in his unmentionables.

When another knock bore no fruit, she called out.

"Tuliver? Hello? Are you there?"

No reply.

She knocked vigorously on the door and, as expected, it swung inward. The aforementioned archaeologist sat, ot rather slumped, in an overstuffed chair at the foot of the king-sized bed. He clutched some papers tightly in one pale hand. His head was tilted at an unnatural angle and his mouth gaped open, as if caught in a scream. But he was silent and his stocky form profoundly motionless.

Dr. Tuliver, it appeared, had received the ultimate critique.

"A" IS (ALSO) FOR ARTIFACT

In Which We Learn That Sometimes a Rock Is Just a Rock

With no more hesitation than if she were crossing the street, Hannah strode to Tuliver's motionless form and thrust two fingers onto his neck, probing for a pulse. The eyes fluttered, then snapped open, and a familiar leer appeared on that pasty face.

"My dear Hannah, I didn't know you cared." Smirking, Tuliver hauled himself into a more dignified position. He emitted an extravagant yawn. "You really should learn to knock, my dear," he continued lasciviously, "or someone might get the wrong idea."

With effort, Hannah kept her temper, although the temptation to perform one of the more ghastly acts drilled into her by her military instructors was difficult to overcome. She heard herself ask what exactly Tuliver wanted of her.

"Nothing but your well-being, my dear," he drawled. "I just thought that you might care to give me a little help, a little collegial aid, on a piece of research that I have out in . . . well, out in the wild West, shall we say. There are certain, ah, aspects of the project in which you may be of use. And if all goes well, perhaps I could be persuaded to pen a short letter of recommendation to the dean. Naturally, I can't promise anything . . . but it could only serve to help with your tenure."

The desire to strike this grinning baboon was nearly overpowering. This was a clear quid pro quo. She was to help Tuliver out of whatever mess he had gotten himself into and, in exchange, he would not oppose her bid for tenure. But what was she to make of his coyness over the location of his site? Did he think she was out to steal his glory? Yes, the fool probably did.

"Suppose you tell me a little more about this site," Hannah asked flatly. "Why do you need me? There are plenty of other archaeologists around." And plenty whose company he'd prefer.

"Well, my dear," said he in avuncular tones, "in this case you may have a particular expertise that is, ah, difficult to come by."

Good grief, she thought. *Was that a compliment?*

"My sponsor, you should understand, is a remarkably public-spirited man. He intends to develop the property containing this site into a retreat center. Not wishing to endanger it by his construction project, he has retained me to excavate it first. But I shall say no more of that until we have come to an agreement. Let us say that if you agree to spend the next six weeks at my site, I shall arrange for comfortable accommodations and a small stipend. Your duties will consist of nothing more than the occasional consultation, so you will have plenty of time to work on that book of yours. And your young friend," he turned and smiled generously at Sean, "I will employ as an excavator."

Hannah could feel Sean's eyes boring into the back of her head. No question what his vote would be. But the prospect of six weeks in the confines of a dig with Tuliver was not how she had anticipated spending the summer.

While Hannah wavered, Tuliver dug into his coat pocket and drew out a Ziploc bag containing several small gray objects—potsherds by the look of them—and tossed it to her. She fished the fragments from the bag and turned them over one by one, inspecting the body and scraping each broken section with her thumbnail to verify the hardness of the fabric. Hannah shrugged. She'd seen a ton of them.

"These are typical Neolithic types. About five thousand years old, give or take. This one's a piece of Peterborough ware. You can see the impressed decoration made by a length of twisted cord. They're all over England and Wales. And these guys are called Grooved ware because, well, they're decorated with incised lines. We found a bunch the season I worked for Guy Sieveking at the Grimes Graves flint mine site. These sherds are rather abraded. I'd say they've knocked around on the ground's surface for a while." She glanced up at Sean, who appeared completely out of his depth, then looked directly at Tuliver. "Sorry to disappoint you, but there's nothing unusual here. So I repeat, what would you need me for? There are dozens of archaeologists in Western Europe who could identify these types of pots for you."

The professor smiled his crocodile smile. "Nothing unusual are they? What if I told you these pots are from a site in, ah, North America? Would *that* pique your interest, my dear?"

★ ★ ★ ★

And so it came to pass that Sean Doyle got his wish.

Washington State isn't exactly Southern California, but it's a hellava lot closer than Illinois and that was plenty good enough. He pushed the button that reclined his seat, causing the nearly empty juice can on the tray table behind him to wobble, overbalance, and drop noiselessly to the plane's carpeted floor. Sean smiled a contented smile born of his good fortune and three cans of Budweiser, which, at twenty-four thousand feet, were having a pleasantly soporific effect.

The uneasiness that he had felt during and after their interview with Dr. Tuliver was dissolving. So what if he was a little secretive about the site? He had the right, Sean supposed. Hannah was making far too much of it. He glanced over at his aunt staring vacantly out the window at the ocean of clouds rolling to the horizon. As she sat, Hannah played with one of her long curls, wrapping it around a finger, then pulling it out like a spring. She was always brooding about something, he observed. Even the plane fare that Tuliver had generously offered them had set her off.

"You think I'm making a problem out of nothing?" she had demanded. "When was the last time an archaeologist paid your airfare? Never. You know as well as I do that contract archaeology projects are run very tightly."

"Except this one," Sean pointed out superfluously. "But isn't this the way archaeologists used to get money back in the old days? From rich guys? Maybe Dr. Tuliver's sponsor is just generous. Seems as likely as the *X-Files* conspiracy that you're cooking up."

"Back in the old days, huh?" she smiled. "Yes, you're right. But the game was very different then. There were only a few professional archaeologists in the early twentieth century. Most were university teachers and the rest worked for the larger research museums, like the Smithsonian or the Field Museum in Chicago—places that have research departments and aren't just there to put up displays. In the very early days archaeologists couldn't just apply to the government. They were expected to rustle up some of their own funds. So they'd go and make their pitches to learned societies and wealthy individuals, drink a lot of tea, and smile a great deal more than they felt like."

Sean closed his eyes and clasped his hands behind his head. Another two minutes and he'd be out for the count. "Sounds like a bunch of politicians raising campaign funds."

"I suppose there's not that much difference. Think of the greatest discovery of the 1920s: Tutankhamen's tomb. Where do you think that the English archaeologist Howard Carter got the funds to run the project? From Lord Carnarvon, a wealthy man who just wanted to be part of a great discovery. And he was! Even as late as the 1960s there were only a few archaeologists outside of academia. Some worked for the National Park Service and others for outfits like Colonial Williamsburg where they helped reconstruct building plans from the colonial era."

"And then CRM was born," whispered Sean.

Hannah jabbed him in the ribs with a bony finger and Sean jerked to attention. "Yep. Cultural Resources Management. Just after the war—that's World War II to you kid—people started to notice that rapid growth had created a slew of environmental problems. The air and water were polluted, and entire species were almost extinct. Well, somewhere, someone figured out that a lot of archaeological sites were being destroyed by the same processes of construction and intensive farming. Archaeology became one of the resources that had to be studied before a construction project could be approved.

"Laws like the National Environmental Policy Act and the National Historic Preservation Act forced developers who needed federal money or approval to identify sites that might be affected by their project, to evaluate them—that is, to see if they were important enough to be saved or studied further—and to dig important sites that couldn't be avoided."

Sean laughed out loud. "Yeah. I've heard NHPA called the National Archaeologists Full Employment Act."

"Well, it certainly increased the demand for archaeologists. I once read that over 90 percent of archaeologists in the United States work in the CRM field."

"CRM *industry*," he corrected. "The commercial archaeology firms even have their own trade association to look after their interests in Washington."

"Really? I didn't know that. Just like the Beef Council. I suppose they have a lobbyist, too. Call me old-fashioned, but somehow the idea of archaeology as an industry makes me cringe. Maybe it's because I'm totally out-of-date."

"No," said Sean pragmatically, "it's because you already *have* a job."

★ ★ ★ ★

The AAA map claimed that it was about an hour's drive from Seattle-Tacoma International Airport to the small town of Vickiesburg where, according to Tuliver, they could pick up the ferry to their final destination, Dougal's Island. Sean slept for most of the trip, reclining at nearly full length on one of the plush rear seats of their rented van. It had not been Hannah's goal to impersonate a suburban mother and her teenage son, but the silver and blue family wagon with the sliding door was the last drivable vehicle in the lot. According to the woman at the Hertz counter, a national convention of well-heeled university deans was in town and had cleaned out just about every rental vehicle in the airport.

They approached Vickiesburg on a narrow and not particularly well-maintained road that followed every turn in the Salmon River. Occasionally a rock slide would cut the town off from the world until the guys in orange from the DOT maintenance station over by Tacoma came to doze the boulders into the canyon below.

The road climbed to a wide, midslope terrace and made a broad turn to the east where the Salmon spilled out into the turquoise water of Puget Sound. Almost immediately the van began to pass a flurry of buildings whose mixture of tourist schlock shops and boarded-up fish packers strongly intimated that this was not a town in the midst of a boom. On the assumption that a ferry was most likely to be found on water, Hannah turned onto a steep road that forked down to the left before a hand-painted sign advertising the Volunteer Fire Department's Annual Pig Roast (only $10.50 and $5.00 for kids!).

Although there was little resemblance between his grease-encrusted coveralls and the sharply pressed uniform of the model in the brochure on his counter, Rick McDonald of Rick's Chevron and Marine Supplies was Vickiesburg's Hertz representative. He accepted the van with a nod and a question about what the pair planned to do now that they were stuck with no transportation at the end of the road. The ferry schedule on Rick's notice board confirmed that the craft was due to leave at 5 P.M., calling at three islands, and returning to the harbor at 9 P.M. Rick, who was also the ferry service's ticket agent, sold them two round-trips to Dougal's with the advice that they might as well buy both ways since there was no other way of getting off the godforsaken place.

★ ★ ★ ★

The ferryboat *Island Maid* had a small glassed-in section ambitiously labeled "The Lounge" with a snack counter and half a dozen vinyl-topped tables and chairs screwed to the floor. Eventually, the *Maid's* diesel throbbed a little louder and a couple of deckhands strode purposefully about loosening lines and ignoring passengers.

While Hannah ambled over to the snack bar to weigh the relative merits of plain M&Ms and those with peanuts, her nephew flipped through an article on the Neolithic pottery industry. Soon, he was deep into the arcane realm of rim forms, shell tempering, and surface burnish. It took three long coughs and an "ahem" before he raised his eyes and realized that a man had taken the chair opposite him and was trying to attract his attention. He was an old man at least in his forties, Sean judged, although his hair was thick and dark. His half smile revealed a lifetime of dental neglect, while his generic jeans and garish T-shirt proclaimed him a thrift store shopper.

"Couldn't help seeing what you-all was reading," he began, glancing at the article in Sean's hands, "and I knew that you had to be a archy-ology student. Am I right or am I right?" Without waiting for a response, the yellow-toothed one held out his hand.

"Name's Claude. Please t'meet you."

Sean nodded lightly and shook the man's bony paw.

"I'm a archy-ologist myself, in a kind of a way," Claude went on without a pause for breath. "Always had a interest in picking up stuff, arrowheads and such, ever since I was a kid. Got a whole bunch of them set in acrylic in the coffee table back home. Real pretty they are." He picked up Sean's discarded article and flipped through the illustrations.

"These ain't much to look at, are they? Now, Al and me—Al, that's my boy—Al and me, we found these . . . well, these arty-facts. And they're something *real* special. Got 'em with me right now if you want to see."

From an old green canvas bag that had once held a French soldier's gas mask, Claude brought forth four lightbulb-sized objects, individually wrapped in white toilet paper decorated with tiny blue flowers. Carefully, the man unwrapped each of the objects and placed it on its own bed of tissue in front of a puzzled Sean.

"Pick 'em up, why don't you," said Claude gleefully. "Just look at that workmanship!"

The stones were gray and waterworn. They may have been basalt but Sean had slept through physical geology and said as much.

The other puffed. "That don't matter, son. Look at the inlay work. Look at them figures. Look!"

Sean rolled the first of the pebbles over in his hand. The stone was crisscrossed with veins of some white material that could have been quartz. It was harder than the encasing matrix and had not eroded as rapidly, leaving a delicate tracery of milky lines. In frustration, Claude jabbed at it with a long finger.

"There, look. Don't you see the old man with the beard? And that looks like a horse."

Each stone, according to Sean's companion, showed scenes of mythical creatures, women with flowing hair, or armed warriors. They were, he was certain, evidence of a lost civilization. Or a way-active

ROCKS O' MYSTERY

Beachcombing on the Oregon coast, Claude makes the discovery of a lifetime. What might look to others like ordinary pebbles are, on close inspection, intricate works of art, depictions of stately bearded kings and a beautiful princess with flowing tresses.

Perhaps, thinks Claude, these are relics of a lost civilization that sank beneath the waves in an earthquake. Museums would soon be beating down his door and he could move out of the trailer down by the river. On the other hand, they might be a handful of rocks.

What do you think?

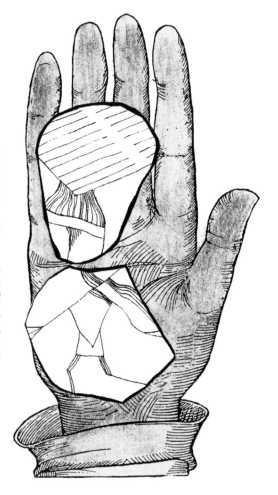

imagination, thought Sean to himself. But not wanting to seem dismissive of Claude's claims, Sean turned the rocks over in his hands trying his best to see the figures amid the random lines. Eventually, by concentrating on some elements and ignoring others, he was able to make out some of the fantastic creatures, although it occurred to him that the process would go faster with the aid of a few beers.

Now, the discoverer of these amazing treasures bitterly told how he had taken the carvings to several universities and museums only to be rebuffed.

"The fact is," confided Claude in a low tone, rerolling his hoard, "these so-called scientists ain't so open-minded as they pretend. The way I figure it is they just don't want to know about any discovery that might go against their own pet ideas, see. They spend their careers working up these theories and don't dare to think of other possibilities in case they're wrong. They've got a nice little club going and they won't let no one in who don't agree with them." Here he nodded significantly and tapped the side of his nose with a skinny forefinger. "But there's one guy I heard about who's digging over on Dougal's Island . . ."

Sean returned the gesture with theatrical emphasis, wondering what kind of a loony-tunes project he had got himself attached to.

★ ★ ★ ★

The *Maid* docked at the end of a long wooden pier that jutted out from the base of Dougal's granite cliffs. It was after 6:00, but the northern sun sailed quite high over the horizon. A deckhand dropped the steel ramp, loosed the chain, and signaled to those who were about to disembark. First off was Claude. With a cardboard suitcase in one hand and his precious canvas bag over his shoulder, Claude loped rapidly down the hundred-foot or so length of the pier and disappeared among the jumble of sheds and boathouses at this, the island's only deepwater harbor. As she followed him with her eyes, Hannah noticed a small form partly secreted behind one of the sheds. The figure nodded to Hannah and touched the brim of its broad-brimmed hat before slipping out of sight behind the rickety building.

Sean shouldered a mountaineering backpack that extended a good eighteen inches above his head. It looked overbalanced and ready to pitch him into the bay. A suitcase on wheels and a laptop computer case constituted his companion's luggage.

"Your friend seems to know where he's going," commented Hannah, hoping that she would have as much luck with Tuliver's directions to the excavation's headquarters.

Sean exhaled noisily. "Hey. I didn't notice you helping me out with that . . ." He didn't know how to characterize Claude and left the sentence unfinished. "I'd never have guessed that you were so interested in fire extinguishers."

"It's always best to be prepared, you know."

"And you were prepared to leave your sister's son alone with Claude the Rock Man."

Hannah stopped to disengage one of the wheels of her luggage that was wedged between two planks.

"Think of it as part of your archaeological education, Sean." She yanked the wheel free with a jerk and they strolled on down the pier. "What was he saying exactly?"

"Mostly about his rocks. And you know, the more I looked at them the more I could see the designs he was talking about."

"So do you believe that the figures are really there or has he just convinced himself that they are?"

The young man scratched his head thoughtfully. "Weeeellll. All the lines he pointed to are real. It's just that there are a bunch of *other* lines as well. And he's ignoring those. I guess I'd say the designs are there but he created the figures by picking out the lines that make them. I suppose old Claude has decided what he wants to see in the rocks and is ignoring everything else. Like Erich von Däniken who looks at carvings of the ancient Maya wearing fancy headdresses and thinks that they've got on space helmets. And that it proves spacemen visited the earth and taught the people how to build the pyramids and those big carved heads out in the middle of the Pacific."

"Easter Island. Yes. I guess he finds it beyond belief that non-Europeans could have the brain power or the organizational skills to build monuments like those. Though generally, the best way is to look for the simplest explanation for an event or a process, since the more layers of speculation you add, the more likely you are to make a mistake. It's an ancient principle called Occam's Razor.

"Of course it doesn't always give you the right answer, but think of it this way: I hear a crash of breaking glass in my backyard. I go back there and find you holding a baseball bat, there's a broken window, and a baseball among the glass. Now, it's possible that the ball dropped from a passing jet, bounced off the fence, and flew into the window."

"Possible but not likely, you mean," added Sean.

"Exactly. Science doesn't deal in certainties, only probabilities. As archaeologists, we dig up the end results of events and processes—like the broken window. We hypothesize about the cause, but we *can never know them* in the same sense that I know a sequence of events I experienced directly. Being wrong is part of being a social scientist. Not that we enjoy that aspect, but most of us recognize that while some types of knowledge are cumulative and build on previous discoveries, some of the models we are attached to now will end up on the scrap heap in a few years."

"OK, but what about something like the theory of evolution? That's a theory, right? But everyone treats it as if it were a fact."

"Evolution is one of those theories that has so much evidence on its side, as you say, we treat it like it was an established fact. But in that way it's no different from many other aspects of life. Listen. We drove down here in a van, right? Did you look under the hood to see if there was an engine there? Of course not. We assumed there was and carried on as if it were there because all we wanted to do was to get to the end of the road. All our observations of the van—how it sounded, the fact that it took us where we wanted to go, every interaction we had with it—were consistent with our belief that there was indeed an engine under the hood. It's the same with the theory of evolution. It's consistent with just about every observation we can make about the natural world. So we act as if it were true even though there is no proof, as most people conceive of proof."

Sean nodded thoughtfully. "When you put it that way, evolution will always be a theory, regardless of how much evidence there is in its favor. But back to old Claude. I don't believe his story about the unicorns and all that junk for one second, but some of what he said made sense. You say being wrong sometimes is just sort of expected.

OK, I understand that in principle. But it's like Claude said. Think of someone who's made his career and reputation on some idea; he taught it to his students, published articles on it, and generally carried on as if it was true. Now, you can't tell me he is going to shrug and say 'OK, it was all for the sake of science' when someone comes up with a theory that is a better fit with the facts. It's just not human nature. No way. He'd fight for his ideas any way he could. And if that's true of an individual, wouldn't it be even more likely if the new idea threatened the careers of a whole bunch of people?"

Hannah put down her bags and smiled at her nephew.

"These are good questions, Sean. But if I talk and carry these bags at the same time for much longer my arms are going to fall off before I run out of breath."

Brushing the loose rock from the top of a low wall, she sat and considered her reply.

"You're asking another good question. Is archaeology self-correcting? That is, if an idea turns out to be wrong or someone makes a discovery that changes everything, will the profession accept it or would some kind of conspiracy develop to hush it up? Did I get it right?"

Sean, who had dropped his pack and now sat on the ground leaning against it, nodded in assent. He felt uneasy about taking Claude's part in the argument but the guy did seem to have a point.

"You'd have to be pretty dumb," she continued, "to think archaeologists have some kind of priest-like devotion to *the truth* with no concern about their own welfare. We're just people after all. We go to the dentist, worry about the future, and paint our kitchens. By the same token, we like to be right and don't enjoy being told when we're not anymore than the next person. It's as hard to generalize about us as any other group. So when Claude says we're all out for ourselves it's about as accurate as saying all doctors order unnecessary tests for their patients because that's how they make their money."

"Some probably do, some don't. That's fair enough. But how does it *really* work? In the archaeology field, I mean."

"You want to hear a story? Sure, I can manage that." Hannah repositioned herself on her makeshift seat and began.

"Once upon a time, back in the 1930s, there was this young archaeologist. He taught at the University of New Mexico and was quite a character. Handsome, dynamic, charismatic. All in all, a guy with a promising future. One summer, this guy and his students were off digging Sandia Cave, a prehistoric site out in the boonies, and they made a series of truly spectacular discoveries—the kinds of things that gets one cited in all the right scholarly publications and generally turn a small-time academic into a celebrity. He found a collection of artifacts he claimed were as much as twenty thousand years old. Now, this was long before the Clovis and Folsom cultures that supposedly crossed the Bering Strait about twelve thousand years ago. The Sandia artifacts were unique and one even looked like a European type of spear. Nothing like them had been found before or since. This guy's reputation was set. And, for a while, all the new archaeology textbooks and articles mentioned Sandia Man. It became as much a historical certainty as Clovis and Folsom."

"Since I've never heard of Sandia Man," ventured Sean, "I'd guess something went wrong."

"You'd be correct. Soon the whole story started to unravel. And here's how it happened. When this archaeologist did his excavation, radiocarbon dating hadn't been invented so there was no way to date artifacts exactly. When scientists came up with the method in the early 1950s, everything changed. Let's just say that questions arose about where exactly the 'Sandia' samples that this archaeologist sent in for analysis actually came from."

Sean's eyebrows shot up. "Are you saying the guy faked his data?"

"I *didn't* say that," said Hannah with great emphasis. "But after the problem with the carbon dating, other archaeologists began to reexamine the Sandia artifacts. Some seemed genuine, but others looked like recent pieces that had been reworked. I heard that one appeared to have been ground down on a grinding wheel!"

"Wow!" exclaimed Sean in widemouthed amazement. "So he *did* make it up."

"I'm not going to speculate on that," said Hannah calmly, "because we'll never know. But I will tell you one thing, which brings us back to your initial question. If you take a look at scholarly articles on North American prehistory from the 1950s onward, you'll find that fewer and fewer mention Sandia as the years go by. And the ones that do tend to waffle about its authenticity by calling it 'controversial' or 'anomalous.' It took a while, but archaeology corrected itself. Not by publicly trading insults or destroying careers, but by simple attrition."

"You mean," translated Sean, "that they ignored it and it went away. Which is exactly what *we* should do unless you want to spend the night on the beach."

★ ★ ★ ★

The evening wore on, and even in those northern latitudes the sun could not be expected to linger above the horizon indefinitely. Hannah fished out the directions Tuliver had printed in small, precise letters on a used envelope. As instructed, the pair took the packed-gravel road inland. Turning right at the first gate, they left the paved surface. The trail was primitive, and the suitcase on wheels bounced and snagged in the rutted surface. Hannah and Sean paused at the top of the rise, and while the aunt rested on a boulder and dug a piece of gravel out of her shoe, Sean dumped his pack and scrambled up a rocky outcrop. From this vantage point, Dougal's Island was revealed as a rolling piece of real estate, mostly covered with a softwood forest that opened up here and there into broad, wet meadows, and divided down the center by a range of rocky prominences. Their path led east around one such meadow, then through a gap in the hills.

The shadows were long now and the line of rock ahead looked almost like fallen castle walls, battlements that had crumbled either from an attack or the decay that comes as the natural partner of old age. Here, in the failing light, it wasn't so hard to visualize the mythic civilization concocted by Claude the Rock Man. Sean scanned the long outcrop, noticing how the shadows built doorways and battlements; how a half-fallen pine draped with hanging moss took on the look of one of Tolkien's "ent" creatures; how a trick of light created the impression of a human form spread out on a large flat rock near the base of the hills.

Sean leaped from his perch and with long strides took off across the meadow like a sprinter. Focusing on a pair of towering rocks that flanked the figure, he charged through the meadow's boggy interior, soaking his boots in mud that smelled of earthy decay. At the far side

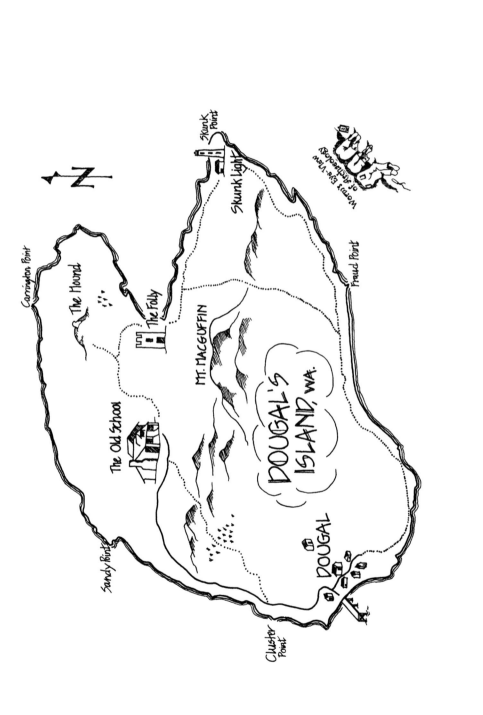

of the bog, he slowed, less sure of himself or what he might find. Would it be an injured climber? Or just a pattern of rocks?

Or, lying perfectly still and clothed in ethereal white, the most awesomely beautiful girl he'd ever seen.

Her eyes opened. She raised herself on one delicate elbow and spoke with the voice of a cooing dove.

"And just what the hell are *you* staring at, goon boy?"

Sean was in love.

"B" IS FOR BINFORD

In Which We Learn What's New about Archaeology

"Are you dumb as well as ugly?" demanded The Vision.

On some level, Sean was aware that he was being questioned. But somehow he couldn't wrench his attention from how the failing sunlight lit up the red-blond hair that poured in ringlets over the girl's shoulder. Freckles had never looked so good.

"Well?" She clipped his shoulder hard with the heel of her perfect hand and he staggered backwards, tripped over a moss-covered boulder, and sat heavily and with little dignity on the gravelly ground. His T-shirted arm raked across the rock's jagged surface and tiny lines of blood oozed from the surgically thin, parallel scrapes, forming droplets that ran down his elbow. Not that Sean noticed. He opened his mouth to reply but could only come out with a series of throaty noises.

Meanwhile The Vision had pulled her lovely self upright and swung her legs around so that they hung over the edge of the flat rock. She slipped her feet into a pair of sandals and stood up, hands on hips, glaring fiercely at Sean who lay in his pile of confusion, tiny rivulets of blood streaming down his elbow into the dirt.

"I . . . ah, didn't . . . ," he burbled. "I didn't mean to . . . I thought you were . . . someone was hurt or something."

"Well I'm not," she said fiercely. And then, seeing less danger and more slapstick in her would-be rescuer's pose, she backed up to a crooked frown.

"You can get up now," offered The Vision. "Just stay over there."

Sean shuffled meekly to his feet and winced as he extended his bloody arm.

"Listen, I'm real sorry if I scared you," he began, picking a piece of gravel out of his elbow.

"Hey, goon boy, what gave you the idea I was scared?" she demanded. "You just surprised me, that's all. I was in a second-level state or I would have heard you coming."

Now, Sean had no idea what a "second-level state" might be—nor a first-level, for that matter—and was about to inquire when a horn blast sounded from somewhere in the middle distance. The Vision's elegant head turned slightly as if to better hear the trumpeting sound. She bent to brush a few stray specks of red dirt from the hem of her robe.

"Gotta go," she said, and clambered around the large flat stone where Sean had discovered her. Turning, The Vision tucked some wayward locks behind her perfect ear and gave Sean the gift of a fleeting smile. "I'm Freya," she said, disappearing into the rocks. "Don't suppose I'll see you again, goon boy."

★ ★ ★ ★

"Now tell me again," insisted the aunt, "that you haven't been smoking that wacko weed." Urged by an instinct that a sociobiologist may have interpreted as a desire to protect her kin group's genes, Hannah had cautiously made her way around the bog through which her sister's impetuous son had so recklessly scampered to find him quite alone and bleeding.

"You must admit," said she, applying the first of a patchwork of Band-Aids to Sean's torn arm, "it's a pretty wild story: A beautiful goddess who dematerializes at the sound of the shofar." Although it was hardly out of keeping with what she knew of Sean's romantic imagination.

"I didn't say it was a shofar. Just a horn. And she didn't disappear, she sort of left." Sean was hurt, and not only by the scrape on his arm. But somehow neither his aunt's playful sarcasm nor her medical ministrations seemed to matter. He had been in the presence of

perfection and even in The Vision's rejection found fuel for a fantasy
of requited love.

The remainder of their walk to the dig's headquarters was un-
eventful and the two kept their thoughts to themselves: Hannah concentrating on Tuliver's directions, which were, thankfully, as precise as
the letters of his tiny printing; and Sean, so distracted by his encounter with The Vision that he would cheerfully have followed his
leader off of a cliff had she led them to one.

And so it was that the pair arrived at the imposing wrought–iron
gate and graveled driveway of the New Magick Retreat Center—or
the Summerfield School as the chipped and blistered sign had announced for the last sixty years.

It is probably unnecessary to say much about Eugenia Rubicon-
Bott, the late founder of Summerfield, for the erudite reader will
surely be familiar with that great woman's contributions to the education of girls. It is enough to mention that from 1905 until 1943, the
school was well known in the most progressive circles for its programs
in art, theater, and Jungian psychology. Shortly after the inconve-
nience known as World War II forced her to put up the shutters, the
founder went into decline. Mrs. Rubicon-Bott was buried on her
beloved island on Christmas Eve 1943.

The old place was invisible from the road, hidden behind a dense
yew hedge and a sweeping curve in the driveway. The wheels on
Hannah's suitcase sunk into the loosely packed gravel. She dragged it
unceremoniously, leaving in her wake a deep gouge like the spoor of
a giant snail.

When the yew and lush privet bushes ended, our travelers emerged
from the gloom and took their first view of the building that loomed
ominously not forty feet in front of them.

"Wow," offered Sean, looking up for perhaps the first time in a
quarter of a mile.

"Wow indeed!" responded the aunt.

Dark and rambling were the adjectives that came to Hannah's
mind. Deep overhanging eaves, dark shingled walls over a half-story
of rough stonework. The facade was flanked by twin stone-built
towers whose soaring topmost windows would have provided a
spectacular view of the surrounding country down to the bay had

they not been tightly shuttered. Four wooden posts, their rough bark intact, supported a broad porch, giving the distinct impression that the roof had grown like the forest canopy from the trees themselves. Henry Bott, a prosperous building contractor, had constructed the place to the specifications of his dear Eugenia in the avant-garde Arts and Crafts style. The outside had never seen a lick of paint because, as Mrs. Rubicon-Bott had declared in her now-famous dictum, "I will have no lying buildings for my girls. Wood shall look as wood and stone as stone."

"Wow," said Sean redundantly as the pair climbed the porch steps.

A note, written on the back of an envelope and taped to the door, directed the senior of the two to her quarters, but made no mention of her companion.

"OK, so where do I go?" asked Sean of the door.

"If you're the new guy on the crew, you can follow me," came a bored voice from the shadows. A slight male figure rose from his seat on the porch railing. "I am Alasdair Crisp, the associate field director. Dr. Tuliver asked me to look out for you, and I've been waiting here since 6:30." The welcoming committee was not amused, and it was clear that Sean had not just found his soul mate.

"We got a bit sidetracked . . ." Sean began apologetically, but was interrupted by their host who flung open the door without a glance at either of the newcomers.

"Well, you'd better come this way," said Alasdair and stalked inside.

Sean looked at Hannah and shrugged.

"Guess I'll see you later. Perhaps," he added over his shoulder, "I'll get Mr. Happy to tell me where the kitchen is and we can get something to eat." Now there was an idea.

"Fine. Let's meet at my room in a few minutes."

Ahead, twin staircases curved gracefully to a balcony. But Hannah did not go that way. Following directions and expecting the worse, she dragged her luggage into the wide hallway, through a pair of double doors, and into a large bare room with a stage at the far end. Rock music pounded from a pair of tiny speakers attached to a CD player that sat on the edge of a table just in front of the stage. The archaeologist's quarters, stated the note, was the right-side dressing room. Finding that the door to her abode was stuck, the new resident applied her shoulder. The door yielded on the second try, and Hannah stumbled into the room and found herself face-to-face with a wild-haired woman moving rapidly toward her. Her adrenaline surged momentarily until she recognized her own image. From waist height to ceiling, the far wall was one continuous mirror where student actors of past years had applied their makeup.

How absurd, she chuckled, to be scared by your own reflection. But such a face!

She glowered menacingly at herself and tried to pat down the ringlets, which, buffeted by the wind on the crossing and curled even tighter by the ambient moistness of the Pacific northwest, now sprung like an unruly halo around her head.

Small and windowless, but with the unexpected luxury of what a sign announced to be the door of an attached bathroom, this was better than Hannah had dared to hope, and she smiled in quiet relief. She rattled the door of the putative bathroom, found it stuck, and decided to try again later.

Now, the intelligent reader may feel that others of our protagonist's age and station would have been less than elated by such meager accommodations; and this your author will admit. However, Hannah's standard of comfort was influenced by twenty-five years of military quarters and archaeological field camps, neither of which are much known for an extravagant regard for personal ease. With a bit of cleaning, thought she, the place would do just fine—although a real bed to go with the mattress would be a nice touch. Hannah hummed along as the CD player began booming out "Purple Haze," a familiar old Jimi Hendrix track.

Behind the door, she found a makeshift clothesline consisting of a length of rope tied between two sturdy nails driven into opposite walls. The previous tenant had obligingly left a couple of rusty, wire coat hangers dangling there, which the new resident appropriated for her black, going-to-meetings blazer and a white cotton shirt that had survived the trip with only minimal wrinkles because of their owner's skillful packing. Thinking the hangers were a little too rusty to use with her one respectable shirt, Hannah fished around for some clean paper in a promiscuous heap of debris left, no doubt, by the former lodger.

Among the torn and wrinkled posters, dusty membership fliers for a couple of archaeological organizations, and grease-stained lunch bags was a one-inch sheaf of white paper held with a heavy-duty clip. She flipped the stack over and grasped its identity from the formal title page and blank signature line even before reading that famous line: "a thesis prepared in partial fulfillment of the requirements of the degree of Bachelor of Arts with specialization in Anthropology."

Now, let it be known that nosing unbidden through the edited draft of a senior thesis is like reading the student evaluations of someone else's course: forbidden, but tempting all the same. But since this stuff had been discarded, there seemed no harm and Hannah rationalized her nosiness as professorial curiosity. She quickly wished she had let it lie.

Underlines, double underlines, and exclamation points scarred the paper's white surface like wounds on a soldier's corpse. Every page was flecked with crimson marks, and some had margins full of commentary, tightly packed in tiny, precise capitals, calculated to pierce and tear like razor wire. Occasionally, she came upon entire paragraphs slashed across their vitals with a stroke of the same angry red ink. Hannah tut-tutted with professional disdain. The manuscript hadn't been edited, it had been assaulted.

She was reeled in now and couldn't draw back. Sitting on the floor with her back against a wall, Hannah opened the manuscript at random and began to read.

In a minute or two, she was brought out from her reverie.

"Hello. Hel-lo?" It was Sean, standing in the doorway holding a tray loaded with the requisites for a simple meal. "You know, I've been standing here for five minutes trying to get your attention."

"You have not."

"Well, a while anyway. I've brought some food for us." He squatted down next to her and began to slice a loaf of crusty bread with a knife that was too small for the job. "Must be some hot article you're reading."

Hannah shook her head mournfully. " 'Fraid not. Whoever wrote it doesn't understand much about the history of archaeology. Her advisor let her know about it, too. Brutal."

"You mean, like the New Archeology?" asked Sean through a mouthful of bread and cheese.

"You've heard of it?" She sounded surprised.

"Hey! I didn't sleep through all my eight o'clock classes."

"Just *some* of them, huh? OK then, Dr. Science, tell me all about it."

"Weeeell," began Sean, suddenly deciding that his shoelace needed tying. "I guess this guy Lewis Binford thought it all up in 1962."

"Oh, is that right?" asked his aunt in a tone that intimated otherwise.

"Yeah, sure he did. I'm pretty certain of that much. He decided that archaeologists should be more like anthropologists so he started this idea of the New Archeology. That's right, isn't it?"

As she was wont to do when playing for time, Hannah rearranged the silver bracelets on her left wrist in order of thickness: the plain first, then the sand-cast Hopi one with the tiny piece of turquoise, and down to the cheap wire ring that she had worn since girlhood.

"Well, sort of." She always began that way when she wanted to soften a no. Patting the manuscript, she continued. "This writer felt that way too. But it's not that simple. It's as I said before, archaeology isn't like Major League baseball. It doesn't have a commissioner who can wake up one morning and decide to dump the designated hitter or extend the season by two games. It changes because the people who do it—the archaeologists themselves—decide individually that the change is a good thing. And, of course, not everyone goes along with the program. Some people stick to whatever they've been doing all along. Others take what seems useful to them—such as a particular technique—and leave the rest.

"Binford didn't just come up with New Archeology off the top of his head. It was a response to what had been going on in North American archaeology for the previous sixty years. He just articulated a lot of other peoples' frustrations and suggested a new program."

Sean nodded thoughtfully. "Yeah, I can see that. Anyone can whine and complain about how bad things are, but nothing changes unless someone comes up with an alternative. But what was so terrible about archaeology at that time?"

"That depends on who you ask."

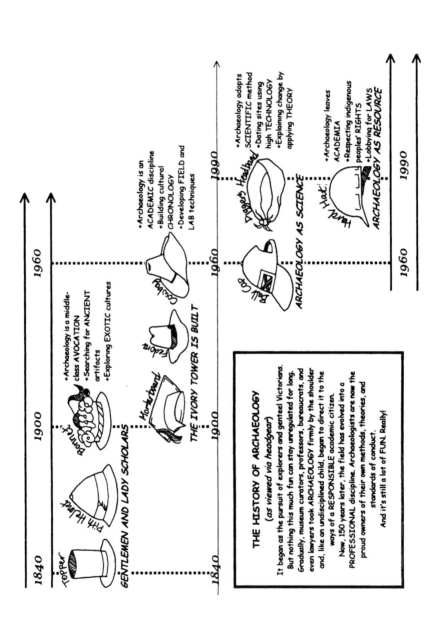

THE HISTORY OF ARCHAEOLOGY
(as viewed via headgear)

It began as the pursuit of explorers and genteel Victorians. But nothing this much fun can stay unregulated for long. Gradually, museum curators, professors, bureaucrats, and even lawyers took ARCHAEOLOGY firmly by the shoulder and, like an undisciplined child, began to direct it to the ways of a RESPONSIBLE academic citizen.

Now, 150 years later, the field has evolved into a PROFESSIONAL discipline. Archaeologists are now the proud owners of their own methods, theories, and standards of conduct.

And it's still a lot of FUN. Really!

1840   1900   1960

GENTLEMEN AND LADY SCHOLARS

Topper

Pith Helmet

Bonnet

+Archaeology is a middle-class AVOCATION
+Searching for ANCIENT artifacts
+Exploring EXOTIC cultures

Mortarboard

Fedora

Cowboy

THE IVORY TOWER IS BUILT

1900   1960   1990

+Archaeology is an ACADEMIC discipline
+Building cultural CHRONOLOGY
+Developing FIELD and LAB techniques

Ball Cap

Digger's Headband

ARCHAEOLOGY AS SCIENCE

1960   1990

+Archaeology adopts SCIENTIFIC method
+Dating sites using high TECHNOLOGY
+Explaining change by applying THEORY

Hard Hat

ARCHAEOLOGY AS RESOURCE

1960   1990

+Archaeology leaves ACADEMIA
+Respecting indigenous peoples RIGHTS
+Lobbying for LAWS

"That's your favorite answer, isn't it?"

Ignoring the gibe, Hannah continued. "Think for a minute about why people studied archaeology in the early twentieth century, when it was just beginning to get a foothold as a legitimate discipline. It was mostly about reconstructing culture history; that is, who was doing what, and where and when they were doing it. In a sense, archaeologists were like historians with trowels."

"And even worse fashion sense."

"Thanks. I'll ignore that. What was I saying? Oh yes. North American archaeologists were mostly interested in reconstructing the sequence of cultures that occupied the continent over time. And they were pretty successful. Think of the important techniques that were developed in the 1900s and 1920s: controlled excavation, taxonomy, seriation, and so on. By the 1940s, archaeologists all across the country had defined distinctive groupings of prehistoric artifacts used by a particular cultural tradition. Archaeologists understood the technology these groups used and how they made a living off of the land."

"Their subsistence practices."

"Yes. In just one generation, these old-timey archaeologists had made incredible progress in understanding the basics of North American cultural chronology. The culmination was in 1939 when old W. C. McKern and his colleagues put several of these local sequences together to create the Midwestern Taxonomic System. And if it could be done for the Midwest, it could be done for the entire continent. It was a great achievement."

"Well, yeah . . . ," began Sean tentatively.

Hannah raised her eyebrows.

"The thing is . . . what more was there for these old archys to do? I mean . . . I know they were great and all that, but if they'd already finished building their chronologies, what were they going to do next?"

"Ah ha!" Hannah poked the air with a gesture that made her bracelets jangle. Here was progress in the education of Sean. "That, boychik, is the point. If you can say that a certain group moved from one place to the next, established towns, developed complex societies, conquered one another, got ahold of pieces of technology—

such as the bow and arrow, which changed what their tool kit looked like almost overnight—if you know all this, what more *is* there to know?"

"That's easy. Once you know what happened, all that's left is to work out why it happened."

"Exactly. Up to that point, archaeologists had kept themselves pretty busy just describing *what* had happened in prehistory. If you had asked them *why* things happened, they'd have given you *historical* explanations and told you all about how ideas move from one group to the next by diffusion, conquest, and by peoples migrating from one place to the next. Think about this: Peoples all across the world, from Mexico to Mesopotamia, developed agriculture independently. Why? What did the places have in common? A few archaeologists, like Gordon Childe, insisted that local economic conditions determined the direction of cultural change. But most didn't think to ask if there were *general* processes—aside from particular historical conditions—behind change and innovation. It's the difference between seeing history as a series of more or less unique events and, as Childe did, as the predictable outcome of a set of social, environmental, or economic forces."

"Whoa! Hold up, Hannah," cried Sean, holding his head. "You're losing me there. What are these forces you're talking about?"

"OK, I'll try it again. You were right when you said that North American archaeologists were at a bit of a dead end by the 1940s. And that is when Walter Taylor came out with his book *A Study in Archaeology*. Many people haven't heard of it, but it predates your friend Lew Binford by fifteen years. Taylor said it wasn't enough for archaeologists to just describe what changes had occurred in the past; we had to *explain* them in relation to a process that is greater than any particular historical context. The approach that Taylor took was a type of functionalism. He saw culture—all aspects of culture—as a mechanism that enables people to adapt to their natural and social environment. Cultural differences, he thought, are essentially caused by subtly dissimilar adaptations to different environments."

"So he'd explain a war as . . . ?"

"A way for people whose population has gotten too big to get more land."

"OK. So everyone started following him, did they?" asked Sean with declining enthusiasm.

"Not at all. Until the Binfords—that's Lewis and Sally—published their *Perspectives in Archeology* in 1962, things went on pretty much as usual."

Sean stood up and stretched. There's only so much archaeological history a guy can take at the end of a long day. "Hey. Mind if I try out your private bathroom before I go?"

"Be my guest. I couldn't get the damned door open earlier. Must be jammed."

Sean rattled the handle and pushed.

"That's strange. I think it's locked from the inside." He pushed harder now, but to no effect.

"Let me try before you break it down," requested the aunt. "It's one of those cheap, push-button locks. They're easy to deal with."

"Deal with?"

"Just watch and learn from your old auntie."

A few moments of rummaging in Hannah's bag produced a trowel worn thin by seasons of excavation and a steel nail file. Using the former as a pry bar, she jimmied the wooden molding away from the door frame.

"Hold this," she ordered her accomplice. "Yes, just enough so that I can . . ." The nail file slid under the molding and bit into the latch. Carefully, Hannah worked the point back and forth until she had forced the latch back into the door. The staccato sounds of Jimi Hendrix's classic "Machine Gun" wafted in; evidently someone had turned up the volume on the CD player.

"Done!" said the amateur locksmith. She pushed the door open and smiled modestly up at Sean. "Another of the little skills you can pick up in graduate school. Almost makes it worth the fees."

But Sean's amusement at his aunt's expertise with a jimmy was swept abruptly from his mind at the bizarre sight revealed through the open bathroom door.

A figure was precariously balanced with her left leg on the toilet and the other on the windowsill, evidently in an attempt to climb through, while struggling to hold on to a large blue plastic basket. She turned and giggled at the amazed duo and seemed about to speak when her sandaled foot began to slide inexorably around the slippery lip of the white porcelain void. There was a shriek as the bathroom bandit fell over backwards and the contents of the laundry basket flew through the air.

Hannah stepped back and calmly folded her arms.

"Welcome," she deadpanned, "to the exciting world of northwestern archaeology."

Chapter FOUR

"C" IS FOR CULTURE PROCESS AND "E" IS FOR ETHNOARCHAEOLOGY

In Which We Learn How the New Archeology Grew Old

As Hannah flipped on the light, the prostrate form groaned and pulled herself upright. She drew a thin hand across her face, smearing blood from forehead to cheek, and looked up at the two like a frightened child. Motioning Sean to stay where he was, Hannah approached the young woman and gently helped as she propped herself between the shower stall and the wall.

"Ohmagawd," said she in an accent suggesting southern California. "This is, like, *so* humiliating."

"You've cut your thumb on the broken window," observed Hannah clinically, "but that's about all." The injured one sat meekly as the gashed digit was bound in a wad of tissues. "Do you want to tell me what's going on?"

"This is, like, *so* humiliating," she repeated, cradling her bandaged hand.

"Let's collect your stuff and go into the other room," suggested Hannah.

And they did.

"This is, like, *so* humiliating," the young woman said a third time, glancing up at Sean and then down at her bandaged thumb. "I was, like, just doing the last of my washing . . . this used to be my room, you know," she added without bitterness, "and I heard you two. I was going to come out when you started talking . . ." She paused for a few seconds, long enough to summon up her courage, ". . . about my thesis and I just had to listen in. And, like, by the time you'd fin-ished . . . it was way *too* embarrassing to show myself. This sounds, like, really dumb, doesn't it? So I thought I'd just climb out of the window. And then I slipped." She gave a weak, hopeful smile and went back to looking at her bloody dressing.

"Ah ha," nodded Hannah. "So it's *your* thesis."

"That's right." The young woman smiled at Hannah and tucked some long blond threads behind her ear. "It didn't sound like you thought much of it," she added shyly.

"Not true," put in Sean gallantly. "I learned a lot about that New Archeology business from what you wrote, Sandy. It is Sandy, right?"

"Sandra," she corrected. "Sandra Beech."

"Of course." Sean realized the significance of his mistake. Sandy Beech would have been, in one very obvious way, quite perfect for this tiny blonde Californian; but it did make you wonder what kind of people would have inflicted such a name on an innocent baby. Al-though Sean had once encountered an itinerant archaeologist called Warren Pease who gleefully insisted that his literary moniker helped break the ice with women.

"Sorry I didn't recognize you, Sandra." Hannah hoped that this wasn't a student from one of her big lower division classes a couple of years ago who had somehow gotten erased from her memory. "Ennui State isn't that big."

"Oh no, Dr. Green. I've never had a class from you. I was a trans-fer student. But I've seen you around campus. Everyone knows you're, like, a long-distance runner or something."

"Or something. You've been working with Professor Tuliver, I suppose?"

"Yeah. I kinda moved over to archaeology from cultural anthro to, like, get more hands-on experience. But it's harder than I thought. Not just gluing artifacts together." She looked down and started rearranging her balled-up laundry in a halfhearted sort of way. "Basically, there's only the senior thesis between me and grad-uation. I've just gotta finish it this summer. There's, like, this job, y'know? Starts in September and they want me to have the degree by then."

"A job where you need a degree in anthropology?" said Sean incredulously. "Are you sure you didn't get a concussion when you hit the floor?"

"Yeah, really!" Sandra pulled her head out of the laundry and smiled shyly at him. "I'm gonna be an assistant research specialist at Recreational Illusions. It's, like, an independent film company in northern California that made the movies about the archaeologist Indiana Joan. They're turning it into a TV series and . . ."

". . . and they want you to play Joan," suggested Sean, privately contrasting the diminutive and nervous Sandra with the tough and buxom actress who, as Dr. Joan, had karate-kicked her way through miscellaneous evildoers and snake-infested jungles in her search for precious relics.

"Hardly! I'm going to help with the technical details. Make sure she doesn't say anything, like, really wrong from an archaeological perspective. That's why I chose the history of archaeology for my thesis." She glanced over at Hannah. "But Professor Tuliver just hates it. I just don't know what to do. And I really want this job. Really."

Sitting on the floor discussing the history of archaeology with a woman whom one has just found flat out and bloody in one's bathroom would be a strange concept for most people. But adaptation to changing environments has been an important theme among archaeologists since the 1930s. And what the hell, thought Hannah. It would be a good way for the student to regain some of her lost dignity. They could take care of the blood later.

"Well, you did make it sound like the New Archeology just appeared out of nowhere," Hannah said gently. "In your thesis, I mean."

"I guess I never thought that it was too relevant to, like, what's going on now. I mean, the early archaeologists weren't really even anthropologists."

"And 'archaeology is anthropology or it is nothing,' right?" quoted Hannah.

"I'm lost," chimed in Sean.

"So, let's go back to the ideas behind the New Archeology, OK? First, you should realize that the New Archeology wasn't just one thing, one standard approach with which everyone fell into lockstep. Archaeology is full of people with their own ideas, and more than its share of iconoclasts. No one is going to just sweep through and *make* everyone give up on their old ways of doing things overnight, or even in a generation. The New Archeology was very influential, but it didn't lead to everyone using the same methods or theoretical approaches."

"Then what did they have in common?" asked Sean in frustration.

"Mostly that they were dissatisfied with the direction the field had been going. What people like Taylor and the Binfords did was to get the field fired up with the idea that it was possible to create an anthropology of the past. That archaeologists didn't and shouldn't be satisfied with knowing *what* happened in the past, they should ask . . ." She waited expectantly.

"Er . . . why it happened?" suggested Sean tentatively.

"That's right! The New Archeologists had an important new goal and looked to the hard sciences for the techniques to make it happen. Remember, radiocarbon dating had revolutionized the field in the 1950s and, naturally enough, archaeologists wanted to know what else these guys had up the sleeves of their white lab coats. And you also have to think about the culture of the era. Post-World War II America was in awe of science. We'd put men in orbit, invented plastic, eradicated polio, and put a TV into everyone's living room. Americans felt that science had all the answers, and many archaeologists . . ."

". . . who—with the possible exception of Alasdair Crisp—are members of human society, felt the same," said Sean.

Sandra giggled and put down the T-shirt she had been folding.

"Right," continued Hannah. "So we dipped into the scientists' bag of tricks and came up with tools like the hypothetico-deductive method and statistical analysis. The New Archeologists also weren't too happy with the supposedly unscientific way that archaeologists connect the data they dig up with their interpretations. Common sense, they reasoned, doesn't apply across cultures. My interpretation of the distribution of artifacts on a site shouldn't be shaped solely by my experience as a modern human. And it certainly wouldn't be the same as someone who lived in a hide tent two thousand years ago. So they concluded that we should study living people and see how they use and discard artifacts, and take that as an analogy to interpret what we find on archaeological sites. That's how ethnoarchaeology was born, and for a few years, hordes of graduate students with clipboards were out there tracking nomadic tribespeople all over the place. Binford himself lived for a while up in the Arctic with the Nunamiut, studying how they used caribou bones. Ethnoarchaeology was the beginning of what Binford called Middle Range Theory, which is really just a way of bridging the gap between what archaeologists find and the behavior that created the stuff."

Sean exhaled noisily. "The Eskimos must have thought Binford was nuts."

"Probably. It's an occupational hazard if you devote your career to picking through other peoples' garbage. But Binford didn't spend his time watching the Nunamiut schlep bones around in the snow just to see how *they* did it. The Nunamiut are only one case of a group with a certain cultural adaptation. What Binford wanted to do was to extend this particular example to cover all hunter-gatherer groups in the past so that he could better understand the real meaning of the remains they left behind. Binford wanted to generalize."

"You mean, like, he wanted to make vague statements?" asked Sean, shaking his head. "Why would he want to do that?"

"No. What I mean is that he wanted to come up with statements about human behavior on the same level as the natural laws that hard sciences are based on. Generalizations in the sense of statements that are true of all peoples everywhere who are at the same level of technological and social complexity; essentially, laws of human behavior."

Sean nodded at this. "Yeah, I've heard that before. But I've never understood how you could come up with a statement that's always true. I mean, people are so . . . different."

"That's right." It was Sandra. She had kept her head down through most of Hannah's monologue, picking at her bandage and tucking the ragged ends under the sides. But now, remembering her own intellectual breakthrough not so very long ago, she became animated.

"It's like this. As individuals, people are, like, unique. But anthropologists aren't much interested in individuals, they'd rather look at whole societies. A lot of anthropologists start out with the idea that all the practices that go to make each culture unique are ways people have developed to help them adapt to their environment. If you accept that, then it makes sense that groups who live in similar natural

Damn you, Lew Binford!
These anthropologists are driving me NUTS

ETHNOARCHAEOLOGY
or
LEW AND THE ESKIMO

An archaeologist digs up a 5,000-year-old stone artifact and says, *"This is a projectile point, an arrowhead."* How can she be so confident? After all, she wasn't around when the object was made and, being dead, the person who used it isn't likely to volunteer much information on the subject.

The answer is ETHNOARCHAEOLOGY—studying modern people who have similar technology for clues about how folks in the past used and disposed of their artifacts.

Lewis Binford is a pioneer in the field. He spent portions of four years living with Nunamuit Eskimo watching how they processed bone into tools. It's true; I swear! Anthropologists are quite an... interesting bunch.

Binford noticed that small fragments of bone accumulated in a *"drop zone"* around the workers, while they threw larger pieces either in front or behind them into what he called a *"toss zone."* Working on the assumption that people in the past had similar habits, the intrepid anthropologist used this information to interpret the distribution of artifacts around 15,000-year-old fire hearths at an archaeological site in Pincevent, France.

environments are going to develop ways of meeting the same challenges that are similar at some deep level. The behaviors are different
on the surface but, in fact, they serve the same purpose: to help the
people make the best use of their situation. What was it that Kent
Flannery said about the New Archeologists? They weren't, like, interested in the Indian behind the artifact, but the *system* behind both
the Indian and the artifact."

Hannah nodded.

"Try that one again," said Sean, puzzled. "Systems of artifacts . . . ?"

"What Flannery meant," Hannah took up, "was that these archaeologists weren't interested in studying *what* individuals or even whole
societies did just for the sake of describing them like an ethnographer
does. They wanted to explain how the entire suite of cultural practices and artifacts is part of an integrated system that helps the society
adapt to its environment. They were seeing human beings as just another part of the planet's ecological system."

"Yeah. Cultural ecology. I sorta remember it," nodded Sean. "So
the New Archeologists were into that, huh?"

"You bet! Of course the idea had been around for a long time, but
the New Archeologists picked up on it because it *explained* things.
The whole model was based on the idea that there's a clear unequiv-
ocal force that shapes all cultures. Cultural ecology said that cultures
aren't just random conglomerations of social relationships, customs,
and beliefs. Each one is uniquely structured to maximize peoples' efficient use of their natural environment."

"OK, but if every culture is so well adapted, why do they change?
I mean, why should they?"

Hannah and Sandra both began speaking at once.

"By feedback," went on Hannah. She pulled out her notepad and,
while they spoke, drew one of her odd diagrams in which recalcitrant
figures in robes and strange headgear were nudged in various directions by little arrows labeled "population pressure" and "food surplus." "If an innovation—irrigation, say—is more effective than the
old way of growing crops, then the people who use it will grow more,
put away more of a surplus, and increase the number of people who
can survive the winter. So their population will grow and the new
technique will spread, and so on."

"And don't forget," Hannah went on, "that past a certain scale, irrigation needs someone in authority to organize digging ditches and to coordinate how the water is distributed between family plots. So before you know it, you have an entrenched social hierarchy. At least, that's what the 'irrigation hypothesis' claims."

"Cultural ecology wraps everything up in a neat package, doesn't it?" said Sean.

His aunt grinned and gave Sean a look as if there was more to be said on the subject. "Yes. And if you'll take my advice, you'll be careful of explanations that seem to account for everything. Cultural ecology is such a powerful theoretical model, but at base it is *only* a model, a story about the way the world works. Like any other explanatory model, cultural ecology can be quite deterministic."

"Deterministic?"

"Yes. Determinism is the idea that a given set of conditions will always result in a certain outcome. It works in chemistry, but people . . ."

". . . are just too unpredictable."

"Correct. Sometimes a random event that has nothing to do with adaptation will change the course of culture history. For example, the army of Ghengis Khan had swept across Asia in the twelfth century and was ready to invade Europe. They were unstoppable. Then, Ghengis died and his armies got recalled. What if he had kicked off a month later? Would we be speaking Mongolian now instead of English? Would the industrial revolution never have occurred? Or the Enlightenment? Would the Pilgrims never have sailed to North America?

"Take it from me, no model explains *everything*. But the New Archeologists made us face the fact that without a model or an approach, we've no place to begin, no way of orienting ourselves to the problem . . ."

". . . or even knowing what the problem is," laughed Sandra.

★ ★ ★ ★

For much of that night, Hannah's bony thighs were gouged by the steel springs that stuck through the antiquated mattress. She had

DETERMINISM AND THEORY

A DETERMINIST takes the position that specific, identifiable factors 'determine' the direction of history and culture, as well as individuals' roles in society. For example, RACIAL determinism (a form of racism) holds that an individual's culture or personality is determined by their 'race'—the physical characteristics that distinguish one population from another. It's hard to see how anyone who has visited a multi-ethnic society could possibly believe this, but many do.

Although human culture must, in the long term, help people survive in their physical environment, ENVIRONMENTAL determinism emphasizes adaptation as the ultimate creator of cultural forms and practices. People are viewed as just another organism that must survive in a hostile habitat. You can think of Karl Marx as an ECONOMIC determinist because he saw all human history as resulting from conflict between social classes.

It's OK to divide the world up for the purposes of study and analysis. After all, we have to categorize influences before we can evaluate them. But to really BELIEVE that human history is driven by a particular force is to deny people a role in influencing the course of their own history and their own lives. It's useful for social scientists to study the world AS IF our models of it are true, but we shouldn't believe that any theoretical scheme can have all the answers.

flipped the thing over and found that the back side was even worse. Finally, she folded her blankets into thirds, put them on top of each other, and slept on the pile like the Princess and the Pea. At exactly two minutes before six, Hannah woke and stretched out her left arm in an arc, encountering the alarm clock at about forty-five degrees. By the use of an uncannily accurate internal clock, Hannah was always—or nearly always—able to beat the thing to the punch. Crappy night or no, she would run three or four miles that morning as she did at home.

Bracing herself against the porch, Hannah stretched out her hamstrings, left leg first, and then reached up and around in a half circle, bending to grasp her ankles. Lastly, she pushed the ever-present silver bangles up her forearm to avoid the clank of bracelets while she ran. A thick layer of cloud—probably ocean fog, she thought—drifted low across the sky, barely skimming the treetops. Occasional wisps curled down near the ground, twirling in mad spirals until they exhausted themselves, condensing against evergreens and undergrowth. It was just as well that she had put her pale gray track suit over the stretchy top and thin nylon shorts. Generally that was all she needed at this time of the year to run a couple of circuits along the creek at Ennui State.

Had she looked up at the shuttered tower window as she ran off, Hannah would have noticed an elderly woman nod several times in her direction and gently touch the brim of her straw hat in an unseen salute.

The runner chose a well-trodden path that might take her in the direction of the waterside, and padded along at an easy warm-up pace. Running a new route is a whole different experience from doing a familiar course, Hannah observed. You have to concentrate. There are decisions to make (like which way to go) so there's less chance of slipping off into that familiar meditative reverie as the legs pump, the arms swing, and the breath keeps time.

Hannah covered a couple of miles through the evergreens and emerged onto a open coastal terrace where the trail split, giving her the choice of either heading down toward the water or back into the trees. She stopped, breathing heavily, hands on hips, and looked out over to the bay. A stone-built tower, perhaps a lighthouse, sat on the headlands. It was really very picturesque and Hannah had made a mental note to check it out at some time during her stay when a flash of light caught her eye. Someone was over there with a pair of binoculars. Or possibly, as her military trainer would have said, a rifle with a spotting scope. She dodged back into the trees and watched for more telltale glints that never came.

Dumb paranoia, scolded Hannah.

She ran on, more annoyed at her own disproportional reaction than the individual who caused it. Hannah had noticed this heightened awareness before, and sometimes it was mighty inconvenient. But there was something about having been shot at during her time in the army that had left the archaeologist with a residual alertness that had little sense of geographic appropriateness. Distracted and no longer enjoying her jaunt, Hannah was just beginning to consider turning back when she tripped and barely saved herself by stumbling off the trail and into the brittle limb of a dead pine tree. A long welt began to rise at her left forearm, just below the bracelets, and Hannah swore extravagantly as she rubbed her injury. She turned, intending to grab the object that had ambushed her so effectively and lob it into the next century, but she found it to be a most familiar item indeed: a wooden pole, three feet in length, marked off in alternating black and white stripes.

She seized the stick and announced in a mixture of surprise and consternation, "You're a goddamn photographic scale." Wisely, the stick made no response, and its restraint was rewarded by being tucked under the arm of its captor, who continued to run in the same direction.

Now, it doesn't take a New Archeologist applying the hypothetico-deductive method to predict that where there's an archaeological scale, there's an archaeological site not too far away. Such was Hannah's expectation, and it was confirmed after a couple of minutes of running.

Ahead, the trees gave way to a small clearing, perhaps five hundred feet across, dominated by a low mound and a huge rock. A single, half-dead pine sapling had managed to get a roothold on the rock's surface. The piles of fine scree that fanned out from its base suggested to Hannah that the tree was only a temporary guest, doomed one day to tumble to the earth as its unsteady foundation collapsed from under it. The signs of an archaeological excavation were all about, though not so different from a construction site to the uninformed eye. To the right was a sad-looking trailer, surely the site office. The boxy structure had once been the home of a family of tourists who had unaccountably abandoned it on the island in 1978. It still bore stickers from a dozen states and one showing the owner's membership in the Good Sam Club that testified to its former life on the open road. A few steps to the left, a three-sided canopy, made from a twenty-foot-long former army tent, sheltered what was probably the artifact lab. Shovels, picks, and other digging tools had been placed without much care against a wooden rack outside the tent, while two or three overturned wheelbarrows and several dozen white plastic buckets formed a heap around a nearby pine stump.

Hannah was in mid-harumph at the unprofessionally promiscuous pile when she saw the first of the upright stones nosing perhaps two feet through the pine needle carpet. Scrambling up the pine stump, her eyes ran from one stone to the next as they circled the mound. A long rectangle about four feet wide had been outlined in yellow string from the base of the great rock toward the center of the mound, and a few inches of soil, the results of the excavation, had been piled haphazardly on either side.

"What the . . . ," mumbled Hannah as she jumped down and approached the excavation. "This isn't . . . right . . . ," she added, stooping down to retrieve a piece of rough, black-surfaced pottery from the back-dirt pile to which she supposed it had been assigned by a less-than-observant student archaeologist.

In a condition somewhere between shock, delight, and disbelief, Hannah made her way from one upright stone to the next. It was as if she hoped to learn from these mossy surfaces how symbols of an ancient European culture found themselves in an island pine forest half a world away. Hannah leaned upon a stump and considered how inconceivable it all was. No wonder Tuliver had been so secretive; if the site was what it seemed, the professor would be an overnight celebrity.

Hannah had stood for a couple of minutes staring up at the back of the great rock and musing over these various paradoxes when she heard the crunch of boots on dry forest cover approaching the clearing. She checked her watch. It was only just past seven, far too early for the excavation crew to arrive. Tuliver hadn't taught an eight o'clock class in years, and Hannah thought it unlikely that he metamorphosed into an early riser while in the field. In no mood for conversation, Hannah slipped behind her stump.

"Do keep it down," pleaded the first voice. "If Dr. Tuliver were to find you here . . . " He left the sentence hanging, but it was clear that the result would not be pretty. There was a familiar nasal quality to the man's speech in which Hannah recognized Alasdair Crisp, her unfriendly greeter from the previous evening. "I knew we should have come out earlier," hissed the voice.

"Now don't you worry, lover," came a woman's self-assured response. "But just for the record, as I recall, it was you who couldn't get his little ass out of the sack this morning." There was some giggling followed by a significant silence and what sounded to Hannah like a hand swatting the back of a pair of jeans.

"There'll be plenty of time for that later," the woman's voice cajoled. "But right now, suppose you get your hand outta there and tell me all about this great discovery of yours? Hmm?"

"It's sweet that you're so interested in archaeology," said Alasdair smugly. Ian Tuliver had an apt student in this one, thought Hannah.

"Yeah, ain't it? Now, about the site here . . . it's from the Stone Age?"

Alasdair snorted contemptuously. "Hardly. The idea of Stone, Bronze, and Iron Ages is quite primitive. Although the general public . . . ," he used the phrase as if it was synonymous with simpleton, "still clings to it."

The woman ignored this gibe, and Alasdair continued in full Teaching Assistant mode. Hannah could visualize the little snot pacing Tuliver-style.

"The Three Ages were devised in early-nineteenth-century Europe to classify sites according to the type of materials found there. At the time, archaeologists thought that human societies evolved through a universal and immutable set of stages, from simple to complex, and that the use of stone, bronze, and iron tools corresponded with these stages. Of course, now we know that this is all nonsense," continued

Alasdair, as if he had personally authenticated the fact to the scientific community. "Just think of the Indians in this part of the West. In only a couple of generations, they changed from using stone tools to iron ones without using bronze at all. Of course, it all happened through the process we call 'diffusion'—by which ideas and artifacts spread from one place to another. That must be how this site came to be here," Alasdair offered vaguely. "Every indication is that it's from the Neolithic. Could be as much as five or seven thousand years old."

"Post-Bandkeramik Period, then," said his companion quietly. But Alasdair, in full lecture mode, didn't seem to hear this scholarly aside.

"The European Neolithic," he continued, "is the period when societies made an increasing use of domesticated crops and livestock, with a concomitant drop in emphasis on wild resources. Populations grew and became more settled; the trend started about eight thousand years ago somewhere in southeast Europe and took one thousand years to get to western Europe and Scandinavia. Archaeologically, we see a widespread use of pottery and ground stone used for grinding grain crops as well as large-scale pieces of engineering such as cause-wayed enclosures, burial mounds, and megaliths."

"Like Stonehenge, you mean?" asked the woman in an innocent tone, which Hannah thought odd, considering the sophistication of her recent under-the-breath comment. "I went there once. The slaughter stone gave me the creeps. I heard there's a place around here where the Indians made human sacrifices and ate them."

"Oh Patty, you are a silly girl," laughed Alasdair, as if correcting a five-year-old. "Those are just stories. No one knows what Stonehenge's so-called 'slaughter stone' was used for. But this site . . . ," and here his voice became breathless with excitement, "is really something different. There's never been anything like it found in North America. It's shaped like a western European chambered tomb—there's likely to be a burial under that mound—and it has Neolithic pottery that has been authenticated by an eminent specialist, Dr. Hannah Green."

Hannah's body stiffened at the mention of her name. Here was the explanation for her presence. No doubt Tuliver planned to rely on Hannah's reputation to support his claims when the inevitable questions arose about the site's authenticity.

"What we desperately need," continued Alasdair, "is a carbon sample so that we can date the site. But that's going to be difficult to find because the acidic soil in this damned pine forest would have eaten away wood and bone in no time. Our hope is that there's charcoal or a cremation at the center of the mound. For these materials," he declared with all the authority of a second-year graduate student, "would have survived the millennia."

Hannah had as much as she could take of Alasdair's pontification. As the student's strangely attentive companion pressed him for more details, Hannah slipped quietly behind the cover of the mound intending to slink out into the woods. But taking one last glance back at the great rock, she stopped in mid-pace.

"Now I know I'm dreaming . . . ," she gasped. For there, carved into the face of the great rock, was an anthropomorphic figure with the faded but unmistakable protuberances of the female form.

". . . it's a goddamned Neolithic goddess."

Chapter
FIVE

"D" IS FOR DIFFUSION

In Which Dr. Green Goes from Diffusion to Confusion

Hannah's head was still swimming three hours later when Tuliver escorted her and Sean around the site.

Her problem, of course, was how a figure with an odd resemblance to the famous "god-dolly" from the five-thousand-year-old Bell Track site in England came to be carved on a rock in Washington State. What was next—an Egyptian sarcophagus? None of it made any sense, and yet here she was looking at the evidence.

It didn't take much acting to convince Tuliver that all this was new to her. How could she not be amazed, confused, and excited even at a second view?

"I just don't know what to say."

"I know, I know!" Tuliver's round face was beaming with pride at the opportunity to show off his site to a colleague. The students, who had been sworn to silence, were only students after all. They couldn't really be expected to understand the magnitude of the discovery. But the awe of a colleague was something to savor. "Isn't it just spectacular?" he gushed in great glee.

The three stood near the point where Hannah had first seen the stone circle and just stared for a full minute.

"Now come and see what's on the other side of the entry stone," said Tuliver, breaking the silence. "You won't believe this. It's . . . it's . . . unbelievable!"

He bustled the visitors to the eastern side of the rock and flung his arms open like an artist displaying a completed work.

"Well? What about this, then?" The little man grinned and nodded his head rapidly. He glanced back and forth between his discovery and Hannah, as if to observe both her reaction and its source. "I believe I'll call it the Washington Venus," he announced.

"Why not the Tuliver Venus?" suggested Hannah mischievously.

"Do you think so?" Her colleague reflected a long moment before giving his judgment. "No, that would be a bit too much."

★ ★ ★ ★

Back in her room, Hannah tried to evict the Venus de Tuliver and everything associated with it from her mind and replace it with a matter of immediate concern: "D for Diffusion."

Oddly enough, the words of the obnoxious Alasdair Crisp had set Hannah's mind to work making this concept palatable to the average undergraduate stuck with a general education requirement. On a piece of yellow, lined paper she sketched out a model showing an odd little creature clutching a hammer who was leaping over similar individuals. She sat down to convert the thought into words.

Yet, the things Hannah had seen that day wouldn't stop creeping into her thoughts. There were basically two ways in which Hannah could account for the site on Dougal's Island: either it was a product of the infusion of ideas from Europe at some point in the distant past, or it was the independent invention of these cultural forms by Native Americans. Or, in archaeological lingo, it was diffusion versus indigenous invention.

Crisp had been quite right about how diffusion—the spread of ideas and artifacts across space and time—had undermined the simplistic nineteenth-century notion that societies must go through a sequence of technological advances that build on previous stages. Isolated groups have been known to move from simple technology to computers in only one generation as they came into contact with people from the outside world.

It's not so much the invention of an idea or a tool that changes the world but rather the way it is spread and adopted by others. Take the

bow and arrow, for example. It wouldn't be true to say that one day
about fifteen hundred years ago everyone in North America was using atlatls (spear throwers), and the next they were shooting arrows—
actually, the former never did go out of use—but knowledge of the
bow spread faster than any other prehistoric innovation that archaeologists can document. As soon as they appeared in a region, arrow
points became ubiquitous, and since the tip of an arrow is much
smaller than that of a dart or a spear, it's easy for archaeologists to recognize. The arrow point is what archaeologists call a horizon
marker—that is, an artifact that diffused widely and rapidly. Hannah
tried her hand at drawing a truck with a cowboy behind the wheel,
thinking that the automobile would be a more familiar example of a
horizon marker. Not so good. She'd stick to arrows.

Since they were unique, the stone circle, the carving, and the rest
didn't constitute an archaeological horizon in Washington State, so
one possible explanation was a single contact by Europeans that had
not lasted long enough to influence local Native American culture.
That's not entirely inconceivable, she thought. For it wasn't so long ago
that historians dismissed the idea of an eleventh-century Norse
colony in North America as fantasy, yet now it was a demonstrated
fact with plenty of hard archaeological evidence. It seems that the settlement in Newfoundland only survived for a couple of generations
and had virtually no lasting effect on the culture of the native peoples.
There had been no diffusion of ideas or technology out of the community.

Even the long-held view that North America was settled exclu-
sively by people who skipped across the land bridge from Asia about
twelve thousand years ago is being rethought. Respected archaeologists are suggesting that there may have been multiple immigrations
in the deep past—including, perhaps, people from Europe. The oldest human remains, like those of the 9,400-year-old man from Spirit
Cave in Nevada, don't resemble modern Native Americans at all. Pre-
sumably, his people were either absorbed into the dominant population or died out, leaving almost no trace of their existence.

*OK, so why couldn't there have been a European colony right here about
five thousand years ago?* Hannah asked herself.

Because, came the reply from her skeptical side, *it's a hell of a lot far-*

ther from Europe than it is from Newfoundland, and—in case you'd forgot-ten—there is no Northwest Passage, so they would have had to walk the whole way.

And surely indigenism wouldn't explain the site. This one seemed particularly far-fetched, since it assumed that, unless there was hard evidence of contact with other groups, a group's culture—and this includes its *material* culture—developed by its own independent invention. It is the radical alternative to diffusion as the explanation of cultural differences and similarities. Was it possible that a native North American group independently developed so many of the traits of people from the European Neolithic? Conceivable, she supposed, but incredibly unlikely.

But the most improbable explanation of all came from the principle of limited possibilities that recognizes that some problems have a limited number of practical solutions. For example, just because people in India and Guatemala use flat slabs of rock to process cereal grains into flour, we can't assume that the resemblance came about because of diffusion or culture contact. After all, how many ways *are* there to grind seeds? But the same can't be said for art and design. Every region on the earth and at every period of history has its own vernacular architecture and art. There are any number of potential ways to use rocks and mounded soil to create a monument as there are virtually unlimited styles of carving. So much for limited possibility.

Hannah was no closer to explaining the site through any of these archaeological concepts. Nor, incidentally, had she made much progress persuading "D for Diffusion" to materialize on the page.

★ ★ ★ ★

Eight hours of sifting soil through a one-quarter-inch shaker screen with virtually nothing to show for it had cooled Sean's enthusiasm for this particular site. Yeah, he knew that it was unique and all that, but finding an artifact once in a while didn't seem too much to ask. There was stuff on the surface all right, but nothing in the mound itself. Digging would have helped break the monotony, and he rightly felt that he could move more soil than Terry Jones, his diminutive part-

ner. But there was no way he was going to annoy her by making that
suggestion. Especially not in hearing distance of the Neanderthal-like
creature who was hanging around Terry's portion of the trench ap-
parently for no other reason than to smile shyly at her. Alasdair had
called the young man Big Dave, for obvious reasons. Sean didn't like
to stare, but the silent one was quite a specimen. He had the broadest
sloping forehead that Sean had seen outside of an anthropology textbook, and his more than three hundred pounds were poured into a
frame about six feet tall. The effect was a barrel on legs.

"You shall work here with Theresa," Alasdair Crisp had announced
that morning after Sean's site tour was over. "If you have any questions, I'll be in the office. You'll find this nothing like those CRM
salvage digs that you're used to—this is a research excavation." He
zipped his turquoise jacket against the wind and turned toward the
sanctuary of the site office.

"Biting sarcasm," murmured Big Dave. "Way humiliating."

Sean wasn't quite sure of the difference and said so to his partner
after Alasdair had strode away. Both activities seemed to involve digging holes in the ground, taking notes about the soil layers, and making sure not to mix artifacts from different proveniences.

"Do they have a-holes like we have here in charge of CRM projects?" Terry asked. "Maybe that's the difference."

Sean laughed. "Is he really so bad?"

All the time Alasdair had been speaking, Terry had been vigorously, even viciously, scraping the ground. At their introduction, she
had given Sean only the briefest of glances. Now she sat back on her
knees and fixed him with a hard, unblinking glare made more intense
by severely short, blue-black dyed hair that framed her sharply
pointed jaw. Terry pulled a brightly colored kerchief from the pocket
of her patched jeans and, workmanlike, wiped the sweat from the
back of her neck.

"That jerk," she growled, and Sean recoiled almost physically at
the woman's vehement tone. "He has no idea what this site is about.
Did you know he's only a second-year grad student? The moron
couldn't dig his way out of a kitty litter box. There are plenty of people on this site who've had far more field experience than him. But
the Lord High Tuliver likes his fancy manners because they impress

that capitalist running dog who claims to own this site. It's frikkin' feudal, the way he runs things here."

His conservative upbringing had left Sean unprepared for this sort of emotional outpouring, and he was quite taken aback. He mumbled something noncommittal and, when Terry released him from her gaze, dumped a bucket of soil in the shaker screen and immersed himself in his labor. Sean decided not to suggest that they trade off digging. The two did not speak again for at least half an hour by which time Big Dave had ambled off to some other part of the site like a giant herbivore searching for new pasture.

By the end of the day, Sean was bone tired. Since he wasn't permitted to actually set trowel to ground, he had screened soil for the excavators. This involved running up and down the trench with thirty-pound buckets of soil all day. Meanwhile, Tuliver's grad students considered the significance of subtle soil changes and Alasdair loudly questioned whether or not the dearth of artifacts was the result of "the new kid's" inability to recognize them.

Sean plunked himself down in an overturned wheelbarrow, closed his eyes, and wondered where the nearest cold beer was located. With his luck, it was back on the mainland. If it hadn't been for the chance meeting with the goddess yesterday, this job would have been a dead loss. He smiled just thinking about her and slowly drifted off to sleep saying her mysterious and beautiful name. *Freya . . . where are you, Freya?*

It seemed to Sean that he had only dozed for a few minutes when his world turned upside down. Someone had flipped his erstwhile couch and he found himself sprawled on the ground looking up at . . .

"Hey, it's you."

"Yep," replied Freya, ungoddesslike in camouflage pants and T-shirt but with a delicate circle of green vines around her head like the crown of a wood nymph. "And now we're even, goon boy."

Sean lifted himself onto one elbow and grinned. "Seems like I'm always looking at you from this angle. Kinda suitable, you being a goddess and all."

Furrows appeared on Freya's brow. "Don't you say that. Specially so close to Her." She cocked her head toward the great rock. "Get up now." She offered Sean a hand, and he was surprised by the strength in that slim arm. And also by the fact that she retained his dirty hand in hers for a few moments longer than was strictly necessary.

"I always come here at this time. After the archaeologists have gone home," she explained, gently. "This is a holy place for us. Come on, I'll show you."

"Us?"

"The Children of Odin."

"Oh, I see," said Sean, not seeing anything at all but following all the same.

"Our camp's over the next ridge at the old lighthouse keeper's shack. We came up from northern California on Wednesday to make sure you archaeologists weren't harming Her." Freya's voice was light and she spoke in a singsong that captivated Sean to the depths, as they say, of his being. "We could feel the vibrations. We knew something was wrong."

Before he knew it, Sean heard himself mumble. "There's a disturbance in the Force, Luke."

But if Freya heard him, she gave no indication. They walked on around the string-enclosed excavation trench to the east side of the great rock.

"There she is," said the girl reverently. "Freya, my namesake. Isn't she beautiful? Isn't she just out of this world?"

Sean drank in the features of his companion's perfect profile. "Sure is," he said with so much feeling that it was obvious even to the worshipful Freya that he was not referring to the stone image before them.

Rather abruptly, she turned and demanded, "What's your name?"

"Sean Doyle."

Freya seemed relieved. "That's Irish, right?"

"Yeah. My dad's folks were from there. Though my mom . . ."

"Did you know," she continued, "that the Irish race are the descendants of Joseph through his son Menasseh?"

Sean recognized this as some kind of biblical allusion but didn't give it much thought, for the analytical portion of his brain was rapidly shutting down; the romantic lad was all emotion and senses. To be alone with Freya toward the end of the day, to be the object of her attention, the one for whom that silky voice spoke. He had to concentrate hard just to keep up the illusion that he was following her conversation.

They backed away from the great rock and unknowingly sat on the same pine stump that had supported Sean's aunt that morning when she was privy to a very different sort of exchange. In soft tones, Freya spoke of the ancestors of the ancient Angles and Saxons, the invaders of Britain, and how they were descended from what she called the "lost tribes" of Israel. She told how this group had wandered northern Europe for centuries and how Tacitus had reported in his book *Germania* that the Germans of the time (who, together with the Scandinavians, went on to invade the British Isles) held that they were descended from an individual called Mannus which, of course, derived from Menasseh.

"Of course," agreed Sean.

"Now Machir was the son of Menasseh," continued Freya, "and his son was Gileath, the father of the Galadon of North Wales, the Galadi-Galatians of Gaul, and the Caledonians of Scotland. And his son—Gileath's, that is—was the ancestor of a group of Saxons called the Haeferingas, whose name we see in the town of Havering in southeast England."

Now, Sean was not so smitten that he didn't realize something weird was going on here. But Freya seemed so authoritative and enthusiastic—and she was soooo beautiful when she was all wound up—that he let it go. Everyone had their own quirks, he supposed. Why shouldn't Freya's thing be ancient history?

"So these folks made it over to North America, you think?" said he, trying to keep the skepticism out of his voice.

"Oh yes. You archaeologists have found plenty of evidence. Hebrew inscriptions on stones in a so-called Indian mound in Newark, Ohio, and lots of other things." She waved her hand as if to suggest the evidence was of such a quantity as to be beyond enumeration.

The Newark Holy Stones? Uh oh.

The case was all too familiar to Sean from an archaeology class. It seems that years ago an amateur archaeologist found a pair of stones engraved with Hebrew characters in an Ohio burial mound, one of which turned out to be a version of the Ten Commandments. The only problem was that they were written in Modern Hebrew, not the language of the ancients. It was quite clearly a fraud—probably commissioned by a local Episcopal priest—although some groups, intent on "proving" their own version of history, still point to the stones as hard evidence of ancient Israelites in the New World.

Fine. But how do you tell the girl with whom you intend to spend the rest of your life that her philosophy is based on poor research?

"You know," he began cautiously, "there are some problems with the Newark Stones."

"Such as?"

"You know how cultures have distinctive styles of artifacts that archaeologists can trace through time? Well, the styles of the Newark Stones are nothing like any other ancient Israelite artifacts. They're unique."

"And that's a problem?" There was an edge to Freya's voice now.

"Well, archaeologists like to have more than one line of evidence," he began gently. "If the Newark Stones were genuine, wouldn't there be other artifacts that sort of resemble them back in the Near East somewhere? Like something in a similar style?"

Freya shrugged. "Don't see why there should be. You archaeologists are always looking to find fault with other peoples' ideas. But you can't deny Her." Freya nodded significantly toward the great rock.

Well, that settled it. There was no way Sean was going to pursue this particular line of argument. It had briefly occurred to him to mention the alternative interpretations of the so-called goddess images: like Alice Kehoe's suggestion that some of the Upper Paleolithic carvings that archaeologists and others routinely say are breasts could just as easily be male genitalia. Especially if you suspend them using the holes that are bored in one end. Or the idea that rotund figures like the famous Venus of Willendorf may have been made by women themselves recording the stages of pregnancy. Realizing that absolute honesty only gets you so far in a romantic relationship, Sean decided to keep his ideas to himself.

"Now you have to leave." Freya's words jerked Sean out of his trance. The fantasy of walking his lovely goddess home through the evening woods evaporated like mist in the Dougal's Island morning. "I have to serve Her, you see."

Freya glanced up at the figure, then turned to Sean and gave him the lightest peck on the cheek. While he was still in shock, the girl stood up and, with arms aloft, walked serenely toward the great rock with more grace than Sean would have thought possible in anyone wearing combat boots.

★ ★ ★ ★

Somehow, "D for Diffusion" had been outlined, taken shape, and was now safely filed away in some cyber-cranny on the computer's hard drive.

Hannah closed her notebook and stood to stretch out the abused muscles of her back. The clock said a quarter to six. Still fifteen minutes before the scheduled crew reception, which meant that she should leave immediately. For as Hannah well knew, if you put archaeologists within striking distance of free food, the latter disappears faster than sand through a quarter-inch shaker screen. Guaranteed.

The tall woman in the long black dress with too much clunky jewelry caused no more than a raised eyebrow as she entered the converted classroom and immediately began piling comestibles onto a paper plate. Each of the crew of four had either seen Hannah on the site that day or had heard, at second or third hand of course, how enthusiastic she was about the project and how certain, how very certain, she was about the absolute undeniable authenticity of the discovery.

She looked around for Sean. Strange to find him absent when there was food to be had. There was the blonde Sandra sitting in an institutionally straight-back chair nibbling on corn chips doused in salsa. Behind the door, the unstoppable Alasdair Crisp lectured Dave, the young Neanderthal whose eyes kept creeping to the televised sight of the San Francisco Giants concluding a three-game sweep of the hated Dodgers. Or perhaps he was more interested in Terry, who was following the game closely from her perch on the arm of an overstuffed couch.

"There you are, Green. Come and meet Mr. Bott." There was no mistaking the voice or the awful familiarity with which Tuliver slid his hand under Hannah's elbow. He eased her over to the side of the room where a grizzle-bearded man of about fifty was sitting in what must have been the room's only comfortable chair. When he rose to greet her, Hannah was surprised to find herself overlooked by at least three inches. And she in her boots, too!

"Mr. Bott, let me introduce Dr. Hannah Green, who is something of an expert on the Neolithic in the western Mediterranean."

Bott took her proffered right hand in his left and held it at arm's length, as if inspecting the goods. He had large, callused hands, more suitable to a laborer than a hotelier.

"Ollie, call me Ollie," he insisted in a rural accent that Hannah just couldn't place. "You've just gone and missed Aunt Alice. Well never mind. She's not much for conversation, is she, Tuliver?" He paused for a few moments, smiling. "Now, now. So you're our expert, huh?"

What kind of bullshit had Tuliver been feeding this guy? Hannah dislodged her hand by turning her wrist against Bott's thumb and backed off a step.

"Well, I'm not exactly an authority . . . ," she began.

"Nonsense. Recognized those potsherds, didn't you?" Bott's tone was commanding; he'd paid for an expert and, damn it, he had better get one. There was a moment of tension. "Now, now. I guess the young lady's just being modest. I appreciate that in a scholar . . . and a woman," he added.

Hannah couldn't tell whether Bott was evaluating her as an archaeologist or as a potential date, and she didn't much care for either. As for the "young lady" crack, well, she guessed that he was no more than five years her senior.

"This is a beautiful old home," she said graciously, "and you have such imaginative plans for it."

Bott smiled broadly, taking the ironic quip as a display of interest.

"Indeed it is. My grandmother Eugenia built the place years ago. Story goes that she'd made a packet on the stock market and put most of it into this replica of the family home out in the west of England somewhere." He gestured widely and let his eyes wander over the dark-paneled room. "She was real fond of this place, Genie was. Turned it into a girls' school, she did."

"Her final resting place is actually on the island, I understand,"

Tuliver interjected, seeking a way to ingratiate himself into the conversation. It was all very well for Green to create a good impression, but Bott's attention was as much his property as was the data from the site.

Tuliver's query was ignored as if it were background noise.

"Now, now," continued Ollie in a back-to-business tone. "So tell me, Doc, what do you make of our little old site. Impressed were you?"

"Well, I'm certainly intrigued," she began cautiously. "But it's rather too early to say . . ."

"Too early?" Bott's voice boomed out and all conversations stopped. Only the baseball announcer's jabber and the distant thwomp of what might have been a helicopter could be heard. Tuliver began dancing a nervous sidestep. But Hannah had never been one to back off from confrontation in archaeological matters and was unimpressed by petulant behavior, regardless of the status of the perpetrator.

" . . . to say exactly what it represents or exactly who created it," she concluded, unperturbed. "I assume that's why Ian is keeping the project under wraps for now."

"Ah. Yes. Well," began Tuliver, who was suddenly conscious of being the focus of every set of eyes in the room. "What Dr. Green means is that, ah . . . we can't be sure exactly what kind of social unit created the mound. Yes, the social unit. Band, tribe, chiefdom, that sort of thing. What do they say about this in relation to the European Neolithic, Hannah?" concluded Tuliver, effectively handing this slippery baton to his colleague.

"I'm sure that Mr. Bott—Ollie—doesn't want to hear a lecture on social structure," began Hannah, but the patron's glare suggested otherwise. "Oh, very well. But be warned: this one has sent plenty of students to the registrar's office to see if the 'drop' period is over." The joke fell flat but Hannah soldiered on. "First, you should know that years ago, social anthropologists noticed that human communities can be divided up into several types based partly on how the group makes decisions or on who's in charge, if anyone."

"In my experience, Doc, there's always someone in charge," interjected Ollie Bott. Clearly, he was used to being that one.

"Yes, but some groups are more egalitarian than others. Look here." She pulled a red marking pen out of her pocket and, resting on the back of the couch, began to draw a series of circles and arrows on a paper plate. Bott shuffled forward in his chair, craning his neck for a better view.

"Here, on the small population end are what we call band societies. People like the Australian Aborigines. They live in mobile groups of a few dozen and make their living by hunting and foraging."

Bott sniffed. "Didn't they used to be called hunter-gatherers? The men did the hunting and the women did the gathering. I recognize politically correct language when I hear it, Doc."

Hannah wasn't going to get drawn into *that* argument.

"No," said she evenly. "If you think about it, foraging and gathering are really two different activities. *Gathering* implies going after vegetable foods, but a *forager* will take whatever's available . . . an animal that's already dead, for example. Band societies move around a lot. They make temporary settlements wherever they go, following the food resources, but they don't wander aimlessly. This month, they may be taking advantage of a fish run, and next they'll be harvesting seeds. From what social anthropologists tell us, their social organization is quite egalitarian. There's no individual that every member of the band looks up to as *the boss*. If there's a job to be done that needs skilled organization—like a fishing trip—the group chooses someone who is respected for that particular skill. But authority is quite fleeting; running the show today doesn't give you command tomorrow. Anyway, using analogy based on these living groups, archaeologists have come to the conclusion that the earliest human communities— the folks who were around in the Paleolithic—all lived in bands."

Bott rubbed his chin thoughtfully and settled back into his chair. "Sound like a bunch of pinkos to me. Don't reckon an outfit like that could organize itself to build my mound."

Hannah nodded, quietly pleased with her success in interesting Bott, who was probably more at home on the range than in arcane discussions. "I think that a lot of archaeologists would agree with you there—at least with the organization part. Before people start building permanent architecture, we see them living in larger groups, say a few hundred or a thousand. I think that you'd be far more at home

RUBBER BANDS AND STATES OF BLISS
or how one anthropologist classifies societies

BAND societies
☞ small mobile groups—egalitarian and kin-based
☞ hunter-foragers
☞ no permanent architecture
☞ e.g., modern Australian Aborigines and ancient Paleolithic peoples

SEGMENTARY societies
☞ groups of a few thousand—basically egalitarian but with cross-cutting social institutions
☞ farmers and herders
☞ permanent towns and religious structures
☞ e.g., modern Hopi of U.S. southwest and European peoples of the early Neolithic

CHIEFDOMS
☞ groups of several thousand ruled by hereditary leaders
☞ fortified towns, sophisticated subsistence system, and long-distance trade network
☞ large religious and defensive structures
☞ e.g., modern Indians of the U.S. northwest coast and prehistoric Mississippian culture

STATE societies
☞ highly populated cities with extensive infrastructure
☞ complex, bureaucratically administered economic system supported by a standing army and judiciary
☞ very large religious and public buildings and religious structures
☞ e.g., modern Britain and dynastic Egypt

with these communities. Most are farmers or animal herders. Social anthropologists call them tribes or segmentary societies. The Hopi are a good, modern example. Each Hopi pueblo is basically an autonomous town, and their societies are quite egalitarian. Although group decisions are made by clan elders, and every resident identifies him or herself primarily by his or her pueblo and clan, all of them are also aware that they are part of a larger unit, the Hopi people."

"Now, now," began Bott, his eyes half closed in concentration. "That's more like it. The Hopi were quite the builders. Their ancestors, the *Hisatsenom*, built Mesa Verde as I recall. Don't doubt that they could have put my mound up if they had a mind to."

Hannah lifted an eyebrow. So, the rough, bluff Mr. Bott throws out the Hopi language name for the people called Anasazi as if it were a matter of common knowledge. Perhaps her first impression of the man was off the mark.

"I'm sure you're right. Segmentary societies can muster a lot of manpower when they want to by getting together with neighboring communities. In fact, the Neolithic people of western Europe who built mounds quite similar to yours are thought to have lived in segmentary societies. Even a small mound would have taken thousands of hours to build, which certainly suggests that people were working cooperatively."

"Quite so," said Tuliver, who was becoming annoyed with the way that Bott's attention was so fixed on his junior colleague. "By the time one gets up to the scale of a place like Stonehenge or Moundville in Alabama, we are talking hundreds of thousands of hours and even more centralized power. Wouldn't you say, Dr. Green?"

"That's right. You see, Ollie, people like the Native Americans here in Washington State and on the northwest coast are quite centrally controlled. Anthropologists call them ranked societies or chiefdoms because, well, they are ruled by a chief. There's a lot of variation, but chiefdoms generally have populations between a couple of thousand and, say, twenty thousand. Their systems of agriculture are well organized enough to create a surplus of goods, some of which goes to the chief as a form of tax. As far as the scale of mound building goes, the big difference between chiefdoms and segmentary societies is that the chief has the authority to organize and feed the hundreds, even thousands, of people working for months at a time that it would take to build a Stonehenge.

"Societies that are any bigger than that tend to have a single ruler or a ruling élite supported by a professional army to enforce the law and to make sure that taxes are collected. It was pretty common for these state societies to have a priestly class whose job was, in part, to warehouse agricultural surpluses. Some of the first bureaucrats were in the state societies of ancient Egypt, China, and Mesoamerica. It's only because they could collect, store, and redistribute vast amounts of resources that the early state societies could build monuments like the temples of Tikal in Guatemala, cities like Pakistan's Mohenjo-Daro, or the massive irrigation system constructed in Egypt during the New Kingdom."

Hannah threw her arms out to suggest the scale of these great engineering works and missed Tuliver's nose by a inch.

"But remember," she went on, "people have been living in all these different types of societies at the same time in various parts of the world. The chiefdom that created Moundville was at its height about seven hundred years ago, while the final stage of Stonehenge was built by a society organized on similar lines about three thousand years earlier."

Bott nodded sagely. "It's like a scale of cultural evolution. At the low end, there's your band people, and at the high end, your people are living in state societies."

"No, no!" To Hannah, this was like lecturing freshmen. She just had to remember not to make it sound that way. "It's not a question of *better* or *more developed*. These are just *different* types of societies. There's nothing intrinsically *better* about any of them. Humans aren't in a race to see who can develop the most complex social organization. Progress is strictly in the eye of the beholder, Ollie."

Bott put his head back and laughed. "Now, now. This is quite the girl you have here, Tuliver." He paused, then turned to Hannah, the smile dropping from his face like a cloud crossing the sun. "But I ain't running no segmentary society here and it's a chancy business to tell the chief where he's wrong."

Hannah wasn't quite sure how to take this remark, but she was excused from considering it for too long as Alasdair arrived with a phone for Tuliver. He held his hand over the receiver and whispered, "It's Jean Grover in Seattle, from the International Geographic Society."

Tuliver snatched the instrument from Alasdair's hand with an impatient, "Yes, I know who Grover is," and turned to face the wall.

Big Dave ventured to suggest that Tuliver had let his subscription elapse.

Even with a rear view, it was clear this was not a happy conversation. The back of Tuliver's bulging neck turned pink and then coronary red, and he let out tiny spurts of air that didn't quite form words. Hannah wondered if he was having a seizure while Ollie Bott looked on blandly, as if Tuliver's discomfort was part of the floor show.

"Alasdair. Turn the television to the Seattle station immediately," ordered Tuliver coldly.

"Yeah, Al. I'm sick of that game, too," chimed in Big Dave, who seemed to have missed the point.

"I don't know which channel . . . ," said Alasdair wretchedly.

"Will you find the bloody station!" yelled Tuliver, adding, "useless twerp," as poor Alasdair clicked rapidly from one station to the next.

Blazing with frustration, Tuliver snatched the remote control from his student, and in a couple of clicks, settled on a newsroom scene where a perfectly coiffed man was speaking against a background of ax-wielding Vikings wearing horned helmets under a title that screamed, "Ancient Site Found on Dougal's Island."

" . . . and now over to undercover investigative reporter Patty Patterson reporting live from NewsCopter 5."

Alasdair didn't hear what she had to say.

Just one look at the face of Patty, his erstwhile lover, and poor Alasdair crumpled into a heap on the floor.

"M" IS FOR MATERIALISM

In Which We Look into the Mind of a Cannibal

As if conjured by Tuliver's fury, a storm front blew into the Northwest overnight. Rain from the Canadian Aleutians pounded the brown shingles on the old school's roof, and the wind moaned gothically through window frames and under doors.

While Hannah Green slept like the proverbial rock on her pile of blankets, the broken window in her private bathroom had not proven to be much of an impediment to the wind-driven rain. By morning, the floor was awash, and the clothes she had worn the previous day lay like sodden rags. Worse still, her black going-to-meetings dress that she had so carefully hung from a nail in the wall was now saturated, having slurped up the rainwater like a sponge. Hannah closed the door. Even her powerful superego could not make a convincing case for dealing with this kind of mess at six o'clock in the morning.

The soggy scene far behind, Hannah ran more gingerly than usual across the damp forest floor, recalling the slip and excruciating sprain she had endured on a rainy February morning out by the creek at Ennui State. Something like that was bound to make you careful, she told herself, but she wanted to run, really run, not just jog along like . . . like someone her age. Turning away from the pine woods at the place where only the day before she had spotted the glint of binoculars, the runner made her way between high shrubs on a narrow path across the terrace that overlooked the ocean. The ground was sandy and drier here, and Hannah increased the rate of her pounding feet to somewhere between trot and canter. For a moment she thought she glimpsed a figure in a broad-brimmed hat out there on the edge of the woods. But before she could focus, it was gone. Must have been light on the trees.

She ran in the direction of the tower, whose crenellated top was occasionally visible to guide her above the bushes that fringed the path. The sound of the ocean was louder now. A muffled roar somewhere over to the left was occasionally punctuated by the crash of a breaker against the cliff face far below.

As the vegetation thinned, the tower came more or less into view. It was of gray stone and perhaps forty feet high. Austere and square, there wasn't much romance about the thing up close. Several adventurous plants had taken root in a crack that opened up from the corner of an upper window and stretched across the tower's face like a great scar. More likely to be someone's paranoid idea of World War II preparedness than anything else, thought Hannah.

Near the foot of the structure, she spotted a blob of unnatural shape and turquoise shade, which caused her to slow to a walk. There was no mistaking that particular garment.

Alasdair was crouched on a rock, hunched over with his head in his hands. Seeing Hannah, he leapt to his feet as if he'd been stung. Hannah gave a wave and ran on, feeling she couldn't very well just turn around. Now, she could see a nylon sheet sticking out like a low roof from one of the tower's walls and the flicker of a campfire that had been obscured by the scrub. But more surprising still was the lanky form of Claude the Rock Man still in his sleeping bag, propped up on one elbow in his makeshift tent, sipping from a mug of something hot.

"Now looky who's here," said the reclining one good-naturedly. He began to peel an orange with a knife that could have skewered a rhino. "It's my friend's mom from off'n that ol' ferryboat. Take a load off, ma'am. Coffee?"

Sean's "mom" trotted to a stop and pushed some escaping curls back under her headband. She grinned recognition at Alasdair, who nodded sheepishly in return with the look of a rabbi who'd just been caught with a BLT.

"The young man here and me, we've been having a real nice talk about the Washington Indians," said he amicably.

"Really?" Alasdair's expression told Hannah that they had been discussing nothing of the sort.

"Cannibals they were," continued Claude. He shoved several orange segments into his mouth and juice ran down his chin.

"Well, sort of," said Alasdair quietly, as if embarrassed by Claude's pronouncement. During his unfortunate encounter with Tuliver on the previous evening, the young man demonstrated his proclivity to bob from one foot to the other when excited or upset. Now, Hannah noted, he was weaving like a boxer!

"Sick sons-of-bitches," stated Claude with finality. His tone indicated little concern with the ethnographic niceties of this practice. "Ain't no other way to explain it. So don't give me any of your 'cultural relativity' horse shit, Al. It gets up my nose the way you anthropologists try an' justify every sicko pre-version by saying that it's all relative."

It was impossible for Hannah just to listen. Rock Man obviously got his information from Rush Limbaugh; one hundred years of anthropological scholarship notwithstanding, it is difficult to argue with such an authoritative source.

"Now just what kind of depravity have you been trying to explain away, Alasdair?" asked Hannah in a mockingly serious tone. Claude's face cracked into a wide grin, showing teeth that would have paid for any orthodontist's BMW as he turned to see how the young man would respond.

"One would have to be a real idiot," went on Hannah after it was clear that Alasdair was not going to offer an opinion, "to think that cultural relativity makes any kind of behavior acceptable."

Claude nodded his approval and tore off another segment of his orange with his teeth.

"No. All relativity means to an anthropologist is that if you want to study or understand some aspect of another culture—such as cannibalism—you'd do well to put aside your own feelings about it. Whether you personally approve of the practice or not. Or whether you'd do it yourself. That way you can gather information about the subject in a fairly objective way."

Rock Man was shaking his head.

"I know what you're going to say, Claude. That people *should* have opinions about whether something is right or wrong. And I don't disagree with you there. Just because in my role as a scholar I may sometimes disengage my personal ethics doesn't mean that I don't reengage them. An anthropologist could study violent street gangs or the subculture of heroin users to find out why they exist and how their members came to be there. But she won't necessarily end up either accepting that gangs are a *good thing* for society or that heroin should be sold in Safeway pharmacies. Of course, cultural relativity can be a dangerous attitude to bring to everyday life, except in the form of 'live and let live.' But as a scholarly technique it's pretty much essential."

"This is one persuasive little lady," acknowledged Claude with a nod in Alasdair's direction. "But seems to me that some things don't need no studying. That good old American common sense tells us what they're all about."

"Like cannibalism, for instance?" suggested Hannah. "Oddly enough, we anthropologists sometimes find it useful to put aside what you call common sense because it's rooted in cultural assumptions. The view of the world that makes sense to the people we are studying—the *emic* view we call it—is only one way to see things. The social scientist can also make up *etic* categories that describe situations in entirely different ways. For example, a person might have a variety of dinnerware in the kitchen cupboard, some of which is used everyday—the 'ordinary stuff'—and some used only on special occasions, called the 'fine china.' We'd call these emic categories. But through technological analysis, a researcher might discover that the two types are made of different ceramic types, have different glazes, and so on. The scientist's technical description, the etic analysis, allows her to compare one household's idea of 'fine china' with the neighbor's. The scientific description might not make any sense at all to the people whose pots she's looking at, but by making up her own categories rather than using theirs, she has a basis for comparison."

"I guess so," said Claude reluctantly. "But what's there to know 'bout folks who chow down on other folks? They do it 'cause they don't know no better. Or 'cause they're starving."

"You've just given two possible explanations. And there are more, wouldn't you say, Alasdair?" Hannah looked hopefully over at the

PUTTING THINGS INTO CATEGORIES

Instead of conceiving of everything as **unique**, people categorize stuff by its most important characteristics according to what they want to do with the information. Confronted with a large dog, the pizza delivery guy is likely to think of it as either "**friendly**" (won't bite) or "**unfriendly**" (might bite). But to a dog breeder the same animal is either purebred or a mutt. Neither pair of categories is intrinsically **better** than the other. Each is **useful** in one context, but not in the other. Get it?

The SCIENTIST classifies animals by their biological attributes: mammals have hair, **birds** grow feathers, and **fish** breathe with gills. Anthropologists call these **ETIC** categories, to denote distinctions that are made by the scientific observer.

Yet, the traditional observant JEW sees the same beasts quite differently. Using rules derived from the Hebrew Bible and other religious sources, he divides them into *kosher* and *treyfe*—animals that may be eaten and those that may not. Distinctions like these, which are used by people in a specific social or cultural context, are called **EMIC** categories.

student, who had calmed considerably and was helping himself to coffee from Claude's enamel jug in a familiar sort of way.

"Oh absolutely," he insisted as if Hannah had made the most banal observation. "In my humble opinion there are some very convincing arguments that explain that cannibalism was actually a response to ecological pressure."

Again, Hannah found herself locking her jaw to avoid sallying forth with a critique, and braced herself against the materialism that she knew was certain to follow. To think that one can explain with such finality the *why* of any cultural practice is the kind of self-deception to which the young are particularly inclined.

He'll start with the Aztecs, she thought.

"The Aztec civilization is a good example," began Alasdair confidently. "Their agricultural economy was based on growing enormous quantities of maize to feed the huge population. They burned much of the land for agriculture, which took away the habitat of the wild game that provided the protein they needed. Unlike, say, the Asian civilizations, the Aztecs had virtually nothing in the way of domesticated animals. The end result was they had an unmet physiological need for protein and fats in their diet. And since there were more humans than strictly necessary to maintain a breeding population, they developed ritual cannibalism as a rational solution to the problem.

"They'd march a prisoner up to the top of the pyramid temple, slice open his chest, and pull out his beating heart before rolling the corpse down the side. Over twenty thousand were sacrificed at the Temple of Huitzilopochtli in 1487 alone," he concluded, as if describing how to make a taco.

"So they worked it all out, did they?" asked Claude, who didn't seem bothered by Alasdair's R-rated description. "That they needed the protein so they'd eat their prisoners? And they made up a bunch of religious mumbo jumbo to justify it to them as was getting ate?"

Alasdair nodded in affirmation, and the two seemed happy to leave it at that when Hannah jumped into the discussion.

"Interesting. But it's only one way to look at cannibalism." Turning to Claude, she said, "Alasdair has given what we call a materialist interpretation. What I mean is, he's looked at the practice with the assumption that it *had* a purpose we can know, some goal to be achieved; and the goal was basically utilitarian—to fulfill some biological need. He sees Aztec society as an entity that made rational decisions to maintain its own existence."

"Like some big corporation laying off workers during slack times to save money."

"Precisely. In fact, that's one of the biggest criticisms of the materialist model. It assumes that everyone all over the world, and at all times in the past, had the mentality of a modern Western businessman."

"But the model works," insisted Alasdair. "It shows a logical relationship between environmental conditions and people's response. Take the 1454 famine in the Valley of Mexico. Nearly half of the population is dying of starvation, and the Aztec priests insist it's because the gods are unhappy with the quantity of human sacrifice. More people are killed, and some of the pressure's taken off the food supply. You don't have to be a businessman to figure that one out."

"True," said Hannah. "But cannibalism and human sacrifice weren't devised to deal with the famine; they already existed. All the priests did was to expand the practice. I'll grant you that reducing the population resulted in relatively more food, but you cannot say this is *why* the Aztecs did it. That's nothing but post hoc reasoning; just because the predicted outcome occurs, you can't know that this was the *intention* of the participants. Wham! Bam! Cause and effect. There's certainly a relationship between cannibalism and nutrition, but it would be naive to say that the participants planned it out or that they were aware of it at all. Sure, eating human flesh may have made some Aztecs healthier, and it may even have improved their ability to reproduce successfully (which in the long run, some would say, is the only important outcome), but what does it mean when we say this is *why* they did it?"

Hannah looked from face to blank face.

"Well, damn it, why *did* they lunch on their people?" demanded Claude in frustration.

"That's my point. As far as the Aztec priests were concerned, they weren't eating lunch at all. They were saving the world. Catholics don't go to Communion to take in calories, do they?"

Rock Man shrugged. "Damned if I know."

"Well, I do. If you asked an Aztec why he was sacrificing another human and eating part of his body, he'd have said that he *had* to do it to keep the world in balance. If the rituals weren't performed, he'd say, the gods would cause all manner of pain and trouble for people. Sacrifice was a sacred event. Human flesh wasn't eaten like a fast-food lunch at a burger joint. Listen. When the Aztec priest was just about to kill the victim, he'd say, 'Here is my beloved son.' And the other would reply, 'Here is my beloved father.' So, in a sense the priest was killing his own child. The same goes for the various Kwakiutl groups here in Washington. Traditionally, they thought of all animals as humans in magical disguise. So when you eat salmon, you're eating a human being; you're a cannibal. To eat salmon is a sacred act to the Kwakiutl. It makes you a part of the great cycle of life and death."

She paused now and wiped away the beads of sweat that had developed on her forehead. Her legs were starting to cramp up. But Hannah's small audience was entirely still, eyes fixed on her expectantly, waiting for the last word.

"What this comes down to," she said, accepting an orange segment from Claude, "is that you can't ask *why* people carry out a certain ritual or cultural practice and expect a single cut-and-dried answer that you can put in a bottle on the shelf and label it '*the one truth*.' Ask a materialist like Alasdair and he's going to emphasize the social *effects* of carrying out the practice—an etic explanation. Ask a culturalist like me and I'm going to give an emic answer and tell you what the ritual means to the people themselves. The two of us are coming from different perspectives, so naturally we emphasize different parts of reality. I'd be the last one to deny Alasdair's point that a society's adaptation to the physical conditions of life determines whether or not it survives. Of course that's right. But it's also true to say that human behavior is more than just a reflection of economic necessity, because it's *culture* that determines *what* people perceive as reality. It sits like a filter between the physical world and people's perception of it."

"Never thought of myself as Jell-O in a mold before," muttered Claude. "But see here, you've got two different ways of looking at this cannibalism thing. How d'you decide which is the better explanation, the mater'alist or the cult'ralist?" Rock Man might not have had much in the way of a formal education, but he could follow a line of reasoning as well as anyone and wouldn't let go until he was satisfied that it made sense.

"To begin with, I wouldn't judge them by asking which one is right and which is wrong," replied the impromptu lecturer. "In this case, there's really no need to choose one over the other, since the explanations aren't contradictory. Rather, I'd think about whether or not they can give insights that are *useful* in helping me to understand this particular behavior."

Claude gave a long, head-thrown-back laugh and began to shuffle out of his sleeping bag, chuckling to himself. As the bag unzipped, his guest was relieved to see the man was fully dressed. A damp waft of sweat confirmed that the jeans and T-shirt ensemble had been his night attire.

"Well now, that was quite a little talk. And I 'preciate you taking the time."

Hannah told him not to mention it. She was anxious to be off before her calf muscles seized up. And what was more, this little sidetrack had given her some ideas for "C Is for Cannibal." Perhaps she could come up with some gory pictures for a cover illustration. That would surely make her editor happy. For every publisher knows violence is a close runner-up to sex on the scale of academic audience appeal.

"And while you're here," continued Claude, ducking into his tent, "let me show you something real special. Seeing as you're so interested in ancient civilizations and all." As the Rock Man emerged with a familiar green canvas bag, his hand grasping something wrapped in a wad of tissue paper, Alasdair groaned mournfully and covered his eyes as if to will himself from the scene.

"Please Dad," he implored. "Not the goddamned Rocks o' Mystery again."

★ ★ ★ ★

When Alasdair failed to show up at the site that morning, rumor and speculation proliferated like flies on . . . well, let's just say that there were a lot of them, and by ten o'clock there were as many theories as theorizers. The most popular scenario had Alasdair loading up his

WHAT HE THOUGHT HE SAID...

"Marry me and we'll... live happily ever after!"

WHAT HE MAY HAVE MEANT...

"Marry me and we'll...
reproduce the existing system of gender roles!"

"Marry me and we'll...
maximize our contribution to the gene pool!"

"Marry me and we'll...
improve our families' social status!"

WHAT DOES IT MEAN TO ASK "*WHY?*"

Ask someone *why* she is doing something and she'll probably tell you her motivation:

I'm hungry. I'm in love. I'm doing the right thing.

But when so many people are doing the same thing that it affects society as a whole, "why" is no longer only a question of individual motivation. That kind of patterned behavior has *outcomes* that affect power relations, social structure, ecological adaptation, and other aspects of society. When this happens, it can be useful to see these behaviors as a way in which a culture makes things happen.

A theoretical model is a *lens* that we can look through to help us see culturally patterned behavior from some perspective. No model can explain everything. But each can give us a glimpse of one of the structures that is behind what we think of individual choice.

Is the *outcome* the reason "why" things happen?

What does it *mean* to ask "why?"

gear at midnight and taking the early ferry back to the mainland in disgrace.

Little Sandra Beech sighed sympathetically. "It's, like, all over for poor Alasdair. Tuliver'll never let him finish his thesis now. How does that country song go? '*An hour's fleshly pleasure brings a lifetime of regret.*'"

"Or ninety seconds' pleasure in Alasdair's case," suggested Terry Jones.

Sandra tittered.

In the absence of Alasdair, Terry had taken command and immediately sent the new guy off to rouse Tuliver and give him the bad news. Following the principle of "shoot the messenger," she thought it probable that the professor would be angry at Sean's report; but the kid was just a digbum so there was little for him to fear from Tuliver's malice. To the rest of them, Terry reflected, Tuliver was both employer and academic advisor—a position of double authority and peril.

Oblivious to his role in the dig's politics, Sean obediently trotted back to the former school, where he found Tuliver and Ollie Bott together enjoying a leisurely breakfast of assorted pig parts, variously sliced, ground, and reassembled. Predictably, Tuliver was not happy with the news, but Bott's presence constrained him from haranguing the courier. He ordered Sean back to the site.

Tuliver made his entrance at 11:15, strolling up to the trench from which Hannah's nephew was extracting a couple of buckets of soil. Now, in Sean's defense it should be said that the buckets were unusually full and heavy and that Tuliver appeared behind him with no warning. The end result was that Sean overbalanced and stumbled into the trench, collapsing a section of its perfectly vertical side on his way down, and spilling his load back into the hole. Terry was about to call her assistant several variations of "dimwit" when she spotted a large flat rock now exposed in the side of her excavation. While Tuliver fumed about the clumsiness of poorly trained excavators, Terry dropped to her knees and carefully troweled the soil from around the slab. Meanwhile, in his theatricals, Tuliver had himself disregarded a basic rule of archaeological practice: don't stand too close to the side of the excavation. A crack developed in the soil at his feet, and the professor jumped back to avoid joining the others in the trench. A huge block of soil sloughed into the excavation, knocking Terry backward and burying her legs in dark clay.

"Ohmygod, ohmygod," she squealed.

"Now don't panic, girl. You're all right," barked Tuliver, annoyed at what he took to be an overly melodramatic response to a simple accident.

"Of course I'm all right," Terry snapped back. "Just look at what's in the side of the frikkin' trench."

The soil had slipped away from the edge of a large slab of rock, evidently the side of . . . something. Above and adjacent to it were wide flat stones—walls and a roof under the unexcavated soil. Sean knew enough to back off, but Terry leapt to her feet and began to probe the void between the slabs while Tuliver climbed down into the trench.

"There's a space here," whispered Terry, "inside the rocks."

Breathing heavily, Tuliver elbowed his assistant aside, and with shaking hands, pulled a penlight from his pocket. It was dark inside the void, and the flashlight's battery was on the weak side, but it was strong enough.

"It's a cyst," he gasped. "A burial chamber. And . . . and . . . there are bones inside." Then he sat back in the anarchy of disturbed soil and began to laugh, and Terry and Sean with him. They in the exhilaration of discovery, and he in the knowledge that Ian Tuliver, a minor academic from a midlevel university, had just found his ticket to the big time.

Tuliver's period of elation was brief, for there were things to be done to secure his discovery. Brushing the dirt from the back of his trousers, the pudgy one gave orders to begin clearing away the loose soil and then almost skipped over to the site office and snatched the cellular phone from its cradle. Mr. Bott would be pleased! Tuliver paused a few seconds, holding the phone, and considered the situation. This discovery had changed everything. Funding was no longer a problem. Institutions would be falling over each other to force money onto him. Although Bott was the landowner, he had become just another player. Things were about to change in their relationship, thought the archaeologist, expanding his chest with anticipation. It was he, Ian Tuliver, Ph.D., respected archaeologist and tenured Professor of Anthropology, who would be calling the shots in the future.

Ten minutes later, Tuliver was back at the side of the trench where Sean and Terry had been joined by the rest of the crew shoveling and bucketing soil. The atmosphere was lighthearted until Tuliver strode up barking out orders, looking dark and ill-tempered.

"Stop at once! All of you, back to your excavation units. And carry on with . . . whatever it was that you were doing. All of you," he added, looking straight at Dave the Neanderthal.

While the others drifted silently away and Tuliver turned back to the site office, Terry scrambled from the trench and leapt fearlessly in her boss's path, hands on hips, like the mother of a defiant teenager waiting for an explanation.

"Well?" she demanded.

Tuliver's anger flowed out of him like boiled-over milk. Far from being excited or thankful, Bott had ordered him to close up the excavation unit and cover the burial cyst! Tuliver had reasoned and pleaded, but to no effect. Bott had even threatened to throw the entire crew off of the island if his orders weren't obeyed. Furthermore, to prevent any more unwanted visitors, Bott had phoned the ferry company early that morning and withdrawn permission for the ship to use his dock until Wednesday, so there was no way off the island. The situation was quite intolerable.

"Well, what does the moron want?" asked Terry, her voice picking up Tuliver's frustration.

"No one in the anthropology department is going to believe this," murmured Tuliver more to himself than Terry. "He insists that we wait until the *International Geographic* team gets here on Wednesday. He wants us to open the cyst on camera!"

★ ★ ★ ★

Lunch time on the site was quite subdued. Tuliver's melancholy had turned the mood of the crew several shades grayer than it was at the moment of discovery. Terry had quite taken her professor's position and wailed about the unfairness of it all. Here was possibly the greatest find since—well, there wasn't anything to compare it with—and it was being manipulated by someone who wasn't even an archaeologist. The site was too important, she declared, to be the property of one person. Obviously, it should be taken over by the government and studied carefully over many years.

"The information in this site belongs to the people," expounded Terry. "It's part of everyone's history. At least, everyone in North America. It's not right that some moron can tell us how we should be doing our job just because he happens to own the land. No one can own the past," she asserted passionately, "it's not a commodity to be bought and sold. It's just too important.

"Information *wants* to be free," Terry insisted. "Take the Internet. It's been a great force for egalitarianism and freedom just because no one controls it. Anyone can get a Web site and put up what she wants. The same goes for archaeology. We should be putting the information, our data, out there for everyone to look at from different perspectives. The alternative is a cabal of scholars—or so-called elders—hoarding the data so that no one can challenge their power. Take the Dead Sea Scrolls."

"OK, I'll take 'em," offered Big Dave with a titter a full octave higher than one would have expected from him.

Terry grimaced at him pityingly.

"The scrolls were kept secret for decades and only a few people were allowed to see them, to study them. Well, it's the same thing here. Power and money are all that's important. The capitalists who have it get to decide what's right and wrong, to hold back scientific investigation, and to decide what the people get to hear."

Terry's monologue continued in much the same vein until she noticed that everyone except Big Dave had melted away back to work. Tuliver was in the site office, Terry sent Sean off to repair the ripped mesh on a shaker screen, and she decided to spend the early afternoon writing up her field notes. Even if they weren't allowed to clean and excavate the cyst she could still take notes and do some photography, she supposed. Terry folded up the blue plastic tarp and sat on an upside-down bucket in the bottom of the trench, leaning against the wall of soil behind her. Her notebook was open in front of her ready to receive her impressions of the morning, but the combination of rising early, a heavy lunch, and the pleasant coolness of the earth at her back brought on a drowsiness that soon turned to head-nodding and then to an out-and-out siesta.

As a rule, Terry avoided midday naps. They always seemed to end in frantic, paranoid dreams that left her feeling groggy, disorientated, and more tired than ever. This time she felt herself at the edge of a deep pit. The edge was collapsing and she couldn't move her feet, as the ground crumbled under her. Just as she began to slip away, there was a voice calling her name.

"Theresa! Are you ill, girl?"

Eyes snapped open. Dazed, Terry just managed to stop herself from slipping off of the bucket.

"No. Fine." She grabbed her notebook from where it lay on the ground, stood up rapidly, and immediately wished that she hadn't as a wave of queasiness welled up from inside. She fought it back. "I'm fine. Just resting. Just taking a rest. Everything's fine."

"Will you kindly stop your babbling?" hissed Tuliver. "Had you been awake, you would know that everything is not fine. Far from it."

A group of half a dozen or so now appeared behind Tuliver and a man stepped gingerly forward, overwhelming the professor with his size and antediluvian appearance. He was profoundly obese and every movement seemed to give him distress. Sean noticed with surprise that two of the newcomers carried rifles slung across their shoulders. He felt it safe to assume (1) that Tuliver had already spotted this particular feature, and (2) that this was not the delegation from *International Geographic.*

The newcomer's snow-white hair was cut severely short, but his beard flowed unrestrained over his chest. He motioned to one of his entourage, a redheaded young woman, dressed like the rest in camouflage pants and shirt. She assembled a portable chair into which he lowered his venerable mass. Sean gasped as he recognized Freya and the two exchanged the briefest of smiles. He also recognized the large man's pained breathing. Emphysema. It had been the same with his grandmother.

The bulky one's retinue gathered around, facing Tuliver as if to challenge him. However, the professor was resolved to stay in control of the situation. They were the interlopers. It was his site and his discovery. He had permission to be here. He was in charge. Tuliver puffed himself up and resolutely returned the leader's stare. In nearly twenty years of playing the game of academic politics, Tuliver had encountered egos of gargantuan magnitude and had generally been able to batter them down. The key was not to allow oneself to be impressed by the histrionic devices with which those egos surround themselves. Although, he noted, firearms were unusually effective in this regard.

"I am Magnus Gluteus, Priest of the Children of Odin," declared the large man as slowly as you would expect from one of his girth. "You have uncovered the bones of our ancestor." Tuliver found himself wondering where they found camouflage clothing to fit the gargantuan form.

"Now, I don't know what you've been told . . . ," began Tuliver.

The large one raised a hand.

"These are sacred remains and are not to be desecrated by your diggings and scrapings. They are not to be tested or groped over. They are for the ground."

He spoke with dignity and a level of solemnity that was disarming. Tuliver could deal with shouting—sarcasm and battles of words were his natural element. But sincerity was outside his comfort zone.

"This is a holy place dedicated to the ancestor who traveled here from Europe to settle this country so long ago. We, the Children of Odin, are his spiritual descendants. We are here to defend his bones." The large one turned to one of his supporters, a painfully thin man dressed like the rest in camouflage green, who eagerly stepped forward and announced that he was an attorney.

"The Children of Odin," he said with gravity, "will file a motion of habeas corpus. Unless you claim nolo contendre we have the resources to respond by appealing to jus divinum. I warn you that ignorantia juris neminem excusat and that we intend to defend our pater patriae in saecula saeculorum!" The lawyer nodded gravely, evidently under the impression that he had imparted some kind of information to the puzzled professor.

Magnus returned the nod and began to speak. After every few words he paused to catch his breath, which added to the sense of anticipation as well as solemnity, for Tuliver expected the whale to keel over at any moment.

"We have not come to make trouble. We understand that you are seekers of the truth in your own way. But you must understand that what you propose is desecration. Our religion is ancient and our beliefs are to be respected. This we insist on. Why should it be that only the Christians and the descendants of Cain are given rights under the law? This we shall not accept.

"And this is not the first time the graves of our holy ancestors have been despoiled by archaeological diggings and their history misrepresented. The ancestor found not far from here was claimed by Indians, and yet your own archaeological tests have shown him to be a Caucasian."

As the large one paused to gasp in some air, Tuliver took up the subject.

"If you're talking about the nine-thousand-year-old skeleton called Kennewick Man, you've really got the wrong end of the stick. It's true that it lacks certain features common to American Indians and Asiatics—like spatulate incisors. But that doesn't prove he was a European. In every population you'll find individuals who don't have characteristics that are the statistical norm. Now, if archaeologists begin to discover an entire population that has distinctive traits, well then, we would be able to give your, ah, theory some credibility."

As he warmed up, Tuliver's confidence began to blossom.

"As it is, there's no such evidence. And furthermore, what I propose to do on this site and with these remains is entirely between myself and the owner of the land, Mr. Bott. I shall excavate them in a scientific fashion, subject them to appropriate analyses, and publish the results. You and your troupe of refugees from an army surplus store will have no say in the matter."

Whether Magnus was breathing so deeply out of medical necessity or restrained anger was unclear. The volume and rate of his wheezing had increased substantially during Tuliver's oration and was causing some concern for his redheaded companion. The girl placed a caring hand on his wide shoulder and whispered gently into the elderly man's ear while the armed men who flanked him fingered their rifles suggestively. The large one nodded and, with a deep sigh and a last glance at Tuliver, heaved himself to his feet.

Big Dave rubbed the stubble on his broad chin. "Fair-sized guy, that," he observed appreciatively.

★ ★ ★ ★

After their visitors left, the archaeologists held an impromptu meeting. It was clear, said Tuliver staring directly at Sean, that someone would have to stay and guard the site that night. Just exactly what that someone was expected to do if anything troublesome were to occur wasn't so clear. Neither was Sean quite certain how he came to be honored with the job.

Having picked the lucky winner in that night's camp-out sweepstakes, Tuliver disappeared back to his office, leaving his crew puzzled and, in Terry's case, angry.

"See?" she demanded. "Here's another frikkin' bunch that thinks it has the right to tell archaeologists what they may or may not study. Here we are with an incredibly important scientific discovery that might just rewrite the history of North America, and we've got capitalists and pagans telling us how we should go about it. It's like I said, they just want to keep the information bottled up. Gaah!" She concluded in frustration, kicking an innocent plastic bucket into the canvas side of the finds tent.

Sandra was swept away by Terry's rhetoric and wanted to say something intelligent and supportive, but she bit her lip instead. She was sure that Terry already thought she was an airhead. Why come out with something dumb and have her suspicion confirmed?

"Yeah, important to you. But some people have different values about that."

Terry turned and glared at Sean. She was not in the mood to be challenged by a mere digbum.

The digbum, however, continued.

"Some people—traditional native people, I mean—think that some information shouldn't be out there for everyone to see. And they don't care if scientists want to know."

"What *are* you talking about?" interrupted Terry in her tone of long-suffering.

"I guess I'm thinking of people like the Hopi clans down in the Southwest. There are some things each clan wants to keep to itself. Like sacred places on the landscape, stories, and rituals. Stuff like that."

"Religious mumbo jumbo," snorted Terry. "Archaeological sites contain important information. You can't have some group telling you what sites you can or cannot dig."

"It is a problem. Couldn't they just let us dig the ones that aren't sacred?" offered Sandra nervously. "Or do they not like archaeology at all?"

"No, a lot of Hopi think that archaeology is fine because it gives them more information about their clan migrations and how they got to be on the mesas where they live now. Not that they need archaeology to confirm that. They already have oral histories and sacred stories. But some places are out of bounds. It might look like an ordinary archaeological site to you or me—only a bunch of pottery sherds and stone tools. But to some Hopi elder it's more than that. Perhaps it's the place where oral history says that two supernatural beings had a battle. Or where the Hopi's Creator told them a story about their origins. So the importance of a site may be more than merely the information that we archaeologists can get out of it. And sometimes that information just shouldn't be out there for everyone to see."

"What about the Children of Odin?" asked Sandra. "Do they have a right to say whether we should be digging here? They have religious values, don't they?"

Terry harrumphed loudly and Sandra knew that she should have kept quiet.

"That's a tough one," replied Sean in a tone intended to show everyone he thought Sandra had made a serious point. "I certainly wouldn't want to say that just because they're not qualified archaeologists they're plain wrong. It's like the Hopi case in some ways. They aren't scientists and aren't interested in how scientists do their work. The same information that we use to work out chronologies and subsistence practices they use for religious purposes. There's no need to say 'we're right and they're wrong.' And besides, Indian tribes are treated as sovereign nations under federal law, right? Congress has already made the decision for us. So it doesn't much matter what you or I think or what any archaeologist thinks."

"If you say so. But that doesn't answer her question," goaded Terry. "Do you listen to the Children of Odin with the same attention that you give to some Hopi elder?"

Sean mused a few moments, thinking of his beautiful goddess. "I s'pose that depends on which one of the Children is doing the talking."

★ ★ ★ ★

That evening Sean found himself pushing twigs into the campfire that he built to while away the period between dinner and bedtime. It was too dark to read, but the smoke had kept the mosquitoes and tiny flying bugs at bay. It was quite pleasant to be out there in the woods all alone with the first of the evening stars just becoming visible. He lay back on his sleeping bag, for it was too warm to get inside, and he began to doze.

Sean could not have slept for too long. The setting sun still glowed over the woods when he sensed soft, fragrant hair on his cheek and the weight of an arm across his chest. It all seemed very natural somehow, and quite wonderful. Without a word, he turned toward her.

"G" IS FOR GENDER

In Which Controversy Is En-Gendered

It was with a sense of foreboding that Hannah began to stretch for her early morning run.

And who could blame her? Both of the previous two mornings she had encountered some kind of weird scenario. It was almost as if she were being manipulated into these bizarre situations by an all-powerful force. Shakespeare might have believed that we are all characters in a piece of cosmic fiction whose entrances and exits are scripted by a capricious author for an obscure purpose of his own, but Hannah Green knew with as much certainty as she knew anything that she alone was responsible for her decisions. And today she felt like running.

She took off at her warm-up pace down the wooded path toward the site with the intention of looking in on Sean. Although the poor kid was getting all the bum tasks on this project, he was taking it all in good spirits and she was proud of him for that. Living and working closely together in less than salubrious conditions makes field archaeologists clear on their priorities: acuity in French structuralism be damned; "plays well with others" is probably the best recommendation that a neophyte can earn after "great cook."

The great rock dominated the clearing while, at its foot, the untidy piles of soil lay like waste from the burrowings of insignificant creatures. Sean was sprawled face down on his sleeping bag by the cold remains of a small fire, as naked as nature had created him. Taking a radical detour to the left, Hannah jogged over to the excavation trench where she planned to make enough of a racket to rouse her sleeping nephew. And this she did, but not for the intended reason.

The excavation was a wreck. A huge, flat stone had been wrenched from the side of the trench and thrown roughly on the surface that Terry had so carefully cleaned of every stray particle of detritus. Soil was strewn around, trampled by heavy boots whose impressions were preserved in the loose dirt. The looters had ripped the flagstone side from the burial cyst and removed the contents except for a few slivers of bone.

The bones known briefly as Tuliver Man had been heisted.

His aunt's squawk of dismay roused Sean enough to open an eye and squint in the direction of the sound. He saw Hannah regard the trench thoughtfully for a moment then dash over to the finds tent. She scampered furtively back and jumped lightly down into the trench. By this time Sean himself was hopping on one leg trying to pull on his jeans, which he found surprisingly difficult to accomplish without the benefit of underwear. He hadn't the foggiest idea what was up. However, he realized with all the perspicacity of one who has been awake for less than a minute that, whatever was wrong, it would not help matters to appear in a condition of total déshabille.

★ ★ ★ ★

The stuff hit the fan at great speed and in prodigious quantities later that morning. And most ended up sticking to Sean. His aunt stayed around long enough to deflect some of the flying flak, but ultimately there was no getting around the fact that the site had been looted on Sean's watch. She asked him how it could have happened. How could he have slept through the looting of the site? But she received only grunts and averted eyes. Regardless, his was the disgrace and he was going to have to deal with the consequences. And besides, other responsibilities were calling Hannah irresistibly.

As late as 10:30 that morning, the elusive "G Is for Gender" existed only as a much doodled-on page of yellow, lined paper. Although she was well-prepared with humming computer, pages of notes, and the mental image of a depleted bank account, the muse of inspiration fluttered off, and Hannah found herself staring fixedly at spots on the wall of her dressing room abode and junking unwanted E-mail messages to the recycle bin. She told herself that the morning's discovery was putting her off, but she didn't really believe her own rationalization. Normally, this was Hannah's most productive time of day and she absolutely would not let it be wasted. The author packed up the laptop, stuffed her notes into a file folder, and headed for the great outdoors. Everyone was out wailing and moaning at the site, so it should be quiet enough.

Set up on the porch with a borrowed table and chair, a mug of strong tea, and a totally blank computer screen, Hannah was ready to start work. Again. And on the cusp of an entirely new set of distractions, the first of which was emerging from the woodland path in front of her.

Alasdair Crisp climbed sheepishly up the porch steps and offered Hannah a tentative smile. So different from the arrogant brat she had met just a few days earlier. For a moment, Hannah regarded the new arrival over the top of her glasses with an expectant expression. Then, to avoid an encore of his nervous dance, she motioned the young man to sit down. Alasdair's embarrassed preliminaries took a couple of minutes before he got to the point, which was to entreat Hannah to intercede for him with Tuliver.

"How are the mighty fallen and the weapons of war perished," quoth Hannah silently.

She screwed up her face quizzically and turned a couple of bracelets on her tanned wrist. "This might not be the best time to approach him," she suggested. "Do you know about what happened last night?" The thought also passed through her mind that a recommendation from Hannah Green might be tantamount to a condemnation in Tuliver's ears.

Alasdair had indeed heard the news and insisted that, on the contrary, this was an especially auspicious moment to tackle the professor, since his own fault was nothing compared to Sean's mammoth screwup.

He was temporarily cowed, but he still had work to do on his tact.

Reluctantly, Hannah agreed to the petition and, for the second time that morning, packed up her gear and stowed it in her bijou residence at the rear of the assembly hall. "G Is for Gender" was on hold yet again. Changing her shoes, she made her way back to the porch where Alasdair was talking to a new arrival.

"The elderly lady in the hat said that Hannah Green is staying here," Hannah heard a familiar voice say.

"Yes. She'll be back in just a minute," replied Alasdair.

The response was three sneezes in rapid succession. Sneezes they were, but hardly recognizable as such. More like small, restrained explosions of air. It was surely how Queen Victoria would have done it, assuming she did it at all.

"Tshh! Tshh! Tshh! Damned allergies."

At the slam of the screen door, the stranger turned around and she and Hannah grinned in mutual recognition.

bd starr was a good eight inches shorter than Hannah, although their weight may have been similar. Hanks of gray-streaked hair peeked out from under a hand-knitted beret of vaguely Scottish hues, and the deep lines around her mouth and high furrows on her forehead showed that this was a woman who offered more smiles than frowns. She and Hannah had been acquaintances since the Middle Ages back in undergraduate school when, prior to a brief marriage to her first art history professor and a life-changing conversation with Germaine Greer in a Chicago elevator, bd had made her way through life as Bambi Denise Starzkopf. She and Hannah still hung out when they ran into each other at conferences.

Hannah didn't have to ask the reason for her friend's visit. The Venus de Tuliver was right up her street, for bd starr was considered something of a rogue academic for her dedication to the field of ecofeminist archaeology. If she had not been awarded tenure in the department of art history at an obscure state college because of her skilled teaching—not to mention her tenacity—bd would surely have joined the bloated ranks of unemployed academics. Typically, bd had not been put off by the lack of ferry service from the mainland. In spite of a profound inexperience in things nautical, she had charmed a dinghy out of dour Rick McDonald, set her pocket compass, and intrepidly motored over to the island, where she now stood asking directions to the site from her old crony. It was decided that the three should walk there together.

"Tshh! Tshh! Tshh! Damned allergies." From the loose sleeve of her blue peasant blouse, bd took a used but carefully folded handkerchief and dabbed her nose. Not a tissue, you understand, but a real, off-white, square of cotton embroidered with tiny red flowers and hemmed with a tiny, precise blanket stitch.

The two women spoke of this and that while Alasdair trailed behind, feeling out of sorts and even resentful toward the new arrival. Events of the last two days had brought Alasdair to the conclusion that Hannah Green was worthy of his company, and he looked forward to discussing weighty matters of archaeological theory with her.

When the friends' conversation turned to the archaeology of gender, Alasdair let out a sound that was a cross between a splutter and a snort.

"I'm sorry," he said in a somewhat patronizing tone, "but in my humble opinion, sex and gender are really modern issues. The lives of people in the past, especially the deep past, were ruled by environmental considerations. Their biggest priority was to organize themselves in the most efficient way to eat and pass their genes on to the next generation. You only have to look at modern hunter-gatherers."

bd turned and cocked her head to one side. "And of course that involved men going out bringin' home the bacon and women staying home with the babies, right, honey?" she offered innocently.

"Er, something like that."

Alasdair felt like he had just walked off the edge of a cliff and wished, just for once, he could keep his mouth shut.

"Matter of fact, honey, there's been a whole stack of ethnoarchaeological studies of the San people who live in the Kalahari Desert that found the opposite. Turns out that although hunting is a high-status, manly-man thing to do, women really bring in most of the food—in spite of having to take care of their children. But if we're going to talk about gender," continued bd, dropping back to walk beside him, "let's start by clarifying some concepts, OK?"

Alasdair nodded without much enthusiasm.

"First, there's sex. Biological sex. Male and female defined by the primary and secondary sexual characteristics. Do I have to go into the details, honey?"

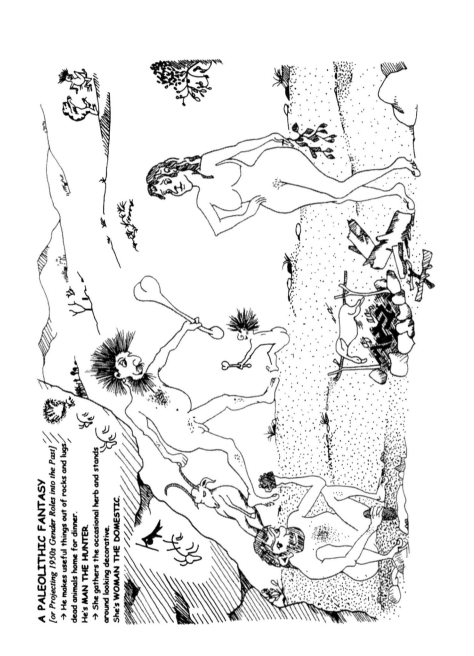

A PALEOLITHIC FANTASY

[or Projecting 1950s Gender Roles into the Past]

→ He makes useful things out of rocks and lugs dead animals home for dinner.
He's MAN THE HUNTER.

→ She gathers the occasional herb and stands around looking decorative.
She's WOMAN THE DOMESTIC.

The young man felt himself color. He looked down at the path and watched the forest floor pass under his feet.

"Then there's gender. These are culturally constructed categories. Every society uses them to decide what's appropriate behavior for each gender. By and large, in American society males don't wear dresses, right, hon? And until recently, the only role for a *respectable* woman was wife and mother. And yet there's nothing intrinsically feminine about a dress or earrings, doing the washing, or working in an archaeological lab. It's just *our* cultural practice to associate these things with females."

"Sure," granted Alasdair, as if stating the obvious. "There are two biological sexes and two corresponding genders."

"Oh really? Ever been to San Francisco?"

Alasdair smirked, but bd was speaking with an ethnographer's seriousness.

"How many gender variations could you count in the Castro District? Men who identify as women, women who live as men, and any other variable that you can think of and probably some that you can't. There are lots of people whose gender doesn't conform with their sex as far as mainstream American culture is concerned. And this isn't just a modern, underground phenomenon in case you were thinking that. There are many traditional societies where the people recognize three, even four genders as easily and naturally as modern North Americans do two!"

"OK, but I don't suppose that's something archaeologists can deal with," shrugged Alasdair.

bd wagged her head to imply maybe, maybe not.

"Without some kind of ethnographic text it would be hard. The Chumash people of the southern California coast, for example, had a third gender called *aqi*: men who took on some of the gender roles of women as well as being the group's undertakers. There's an archaeologist friend of mine, Sandy Hollimon, who thinks that she can identify these individuals by the female-associated artifacts that were buried with them.

"In every culture ethnographers have found that social roles, division of labor, and structures of power are closely related to gender differences. To a large extent, socializing kids is a matter of teaching them the culturally approved roles for their gender. Girls should act in this way. Wear these kinds of clothes. Model their behavior after adults of the same gender. And the same goes for little boys. It prepares them for the roles they'll play when they grow up and become functioning adults. Right, honey?"

Alasdair shrugged. bd reminded him of his mother. "What's so bad about that?" he said. "Without some generally accepted norms you couldn't have organized society."

"Sure. No argument with that, hon. Problem is when our ideas about gender roles—which are culturally variable—get confounded with biological sex, which, by and large, is set at conception. End result is biological determinism: women and men do what they do in society because of their sex. Gender roles come to be seen as 'natural' outcomes of our biological differences. And that leaves half the population . . ."

". . . pregnant, barefoot, and at the cooking hearth," added Hannah.

Alasdair gave a harrumph. "Now you're talking politics, not archaeology." His companions would have jumped in there and then, but he went on rapidly. "This is all very well but what do archaeologists have to do with all this?"

"That takes us to the feminist critique of archaeology," began bd. "Archaeologists have projected the male-headed household back into the ancient past. They wrote about women as dependent creatures who were anchored to their wifely duties around the home because of their children. Conversely, men were independent, coming and going as they wanted, and making all the important decisions by virtue of the fact that they supposedly supplied the food. A lot of archaeologists just assume that certain artifact types, like stone hunting tools, are things used by men, while pottery and textiles—the home crafts—supposedly represent women's work. Here's my point (and don't think I don't see you rolling your eyes, hon). When scientists make statements, they give them authority. People believe the guy in the white lab coat and think to themselves, 'It must be true because otherwise the Expert wouldn't be saying it.'

"So, when some paleoanthropologist comes up with a model of protohuman behavior that has mother Lucy staying home with the kids while daddy goes off hunting game, he makes it seem that these gender roles are actually biologically based—as if it's been that way among humans since before we were human, that it's right and natural that men's and women's roles should be as he says they were."

"Yeah, it's like I said. That's politics. Isn't there a way of bringing women into prehistory without . . . ," Alasdair wanted to choose his words carefully here, "making a feminist statement? Can't you have an archaeology of gender that isn't so much like a political agenda?"

"Sure, hon. That's been done. But you'll find me rather cynical on the subject. We call it the 'add women and stir' approach. If you don't go into archaeological interpretation thinking like a feminist, you reproduce all the old assumptions. Throw in a few references to female contributions and then go on with whatever you wanted to say in the first place."

Alasdair shook his head. "Sorry. I'm just not convinced. The feminist critique thing I get. It sounds reasonable and I'm sure archaeologists will learn from it. But it's only that—a critique. It's not a theory, not an explanatory framework or model like cultural materialism or human ecology. It gets you somewhere in terms of contemporary politics, civil rights, and all that sort of thing, but it doesn't *explain* cultural change the way the great anthropological models do."

"That's a good insight, hon," said bd, resting her hand briefly on Alasdair's shoulder. "And in a sense you're right. But you've brought up the question of what the goals of archaeology should be. Can be. Those kinds of explanatory models work at an entirely different scale than what we've been talking about. The ecological anthropologists and others of the processual school are interested in seeing how history works itself out at the largest scale. How did the society go about managing its resources? How successful was it in the long run? But gender relations are played out on the small stage, in households and families. The two approaches can have quite different goals. Often, they just pass each other by and don't stop to say hello. But I'm not saying a feminist archaeology of gender can't work on that scale. Just that it doesn't have to. Even when women work primarily in the household, their work is important for society at large."

The group paused for a few moments while bd, balancing herself using Hannah's shoulder, extracted a twig from her sandal.

"Do you know Christine Hastorf's work on Inca society?" she continued, flicking the offending woody fragment into the air. "Women were responsible for making corn beer, a very important commodity that was central in the symbolic expression of Inca politics and power relations. By looking at seed remains as well as collagen from human bone, Hastorf came to the conclusion that although they took on more and more responsibility for making the beer, the women didn't get to drink it. So it seems clear that women's status declined through time from the pre-Inca period. And since we're talking about women south of the border, how about Elizabeth Brumfiel? She looked at society in the Valley of Mexico before and after the Aztec conquest. Women were responsible for weaving and cooking. Pretty dull, huh? Well it turns out that the cloth they made, like Inca beer, wasn't just a utilitarian product. It was used like currency. Money. When the Aztecs came in, Brumfiel says the valley cloth wasn't needed much anymore. They got it by exchange from other places in the Aztec empire. So women's labor was redirected toward making foods, like tortillas and dried foods. This says something about women's role in creating the mobile labor force that was so important to the Aztec economy.

"Even though changes in gender roles and gender-linked behavior are played out on the domestic stage, they can have great consequences. Is it worthwhile studying these changes, hon? And how they transformed peoples' lives? I'd say yes. But, from everything I've heard, you don't have to look any further than right here for a potential example of feminist archaeology."

bd gestured toward the clearing up ahead with its archaeological paraphernalia and bent-over workers, and the great rock overlooking them all.

"I'm not sure just what you mean," replied Alasdair, becoming more than a little sweaty this close to his destination, "but if it has anything to do with feminist archaeology, I don't suppose that Dr. Tuliver would agree."

★ ★ ★ ★

From his viewpoint behind the fallen pine tree, Sean could see it all and rather wished he couldn't. It was some kind of ritual, of that he was quite sure, with a lot of hands held aloft, a rather puny set of deer antlers, and a constant rhythmic chant.

"O-din. O-din. O-din. Hear our call!"

Once, a participant made a wrong turn in the group's circuit around the wood pyre that was the focus of their activity and the entire group bumped into each other, one after the next, a crew of white-robed Keystone Kops. Perhaps Sean should leave? He didn't feel right about spying on the Children of Odin, but he'd come to get some answers and to redeem himself in the eyes of the other diggers.

It had been an ugly scene back at the site. Tuliver had all but accused him of stealing the burial himself. Or, at the very least, plotting to do so. Freya's momentary display of recognition the previous afternoon had been captured by Tuliver's discerning eye, and Sean was forced to admit she had returned that evening. But his stubborn refusal to divulge any additional details of their encounter caused Tuliver's anger to boil into a seething mess of accusations and insults.

How had the camouflaged lunatics found out about the burial so quickly unless someone had told them?

Sean had no idea.

How could they possibly have skulked onto the site and dug out the remains without being noticed?

Sean knew only too well, but kept his peace as any gentleman would, and crept away confused and hurt with Tuliver's shouts assailing his back like stinging flies.

The pine branch that had been sticking into his knee for the previous five minutes was finally enough of an annoyance for Sean to reposition himself behind the fallen tree. He was far enough from the celebrants to be unconcerned about the attendant rustling and crackling sounds that would surely be drowned out by the continued chant.

"O-din. O-din. O-din. Hear our call!"

Sean stifled a snorting laugh. This must be why religions have ritual languages—Latin, Hebrew, Sanskrit, and the rest—so that the banality of what was being said wouldn't occur to the participants and cause them to lapse into a fit of the giggles, which would spoil the effect completely.

There was another pileup over at the ritual. The intoning voices stopped raggedly, and someone, possibly the group's Latin-spouting lawyer, was shouting in anger. Instinctively, Sean ducked his head behind the trunk of the great tree.

"Left. Right. What the hell does it matter *which* way I go?" A white gown hit the ground and a figure stomped off. "I'm outta here," he yelled over his shoulder. The five remaining Children were motionless for a few seconds as if deciding what to do. There was some low mumbling and four of the robes trouped off in a group.

Freya pulled back her hood and dejectedly watched them go. She looked around where the horns, the robe, and other accoutrements of the abandoned rite lay forlorn, then stooped to gather them up. It was a most melancholy scene and one that caused all Sean's anger to dissolve and his self-pity to evaporate like mist in the Washington morning. Explanations could wait. He just wanted to be with her, to comfort her.

★ ★ ★ ★

"Oh my gawd, it's the lunatic fringe."

Tuliver shook his head in a give-me-strength sort of way and leaned dangerously far back on his chair. There was barely sufficient room in the trailer for all four, and his visitors clustered by the door. They were not invited inside. In his mind, Tuliver had good reason to detest them all for their respective contributions to his mounting frustrations: Alasdair Crisp, the turncoat; Hannah Green, a flirt whose idiot nephew had all but destroyed the site single-handedly; and that ridiculous bd starr who set serious archaeology back twenty years with her absurd goddess prattle. What a noxious little band of reptiles they were.

"Good morning, Ian, honey. Aren't you going to invite us in?" said bd innocuously.

"Come in and sit down. Do."

Alasdair took the one chair, having never been taught to do otherwise. Then followed a silence that Tuliver refused to break. He leaned back even farther and folded his arms, looking expectantly at bd with his usual inscrutable smile.

"Know what I'm doing here?" asked bd.

Tuliver shrugged. "Can't imagine. Are you, perhaps, changing your area of interest from fiction to archaeology?"

That bd returned the smile, Tuliver found unsettling. It was as if she had a bombshell to drop on him and didn't mind stretching out the time before it was delivered, enjoying the anticipation.

"Oh, Ian, honey, you're such a humorist. Fact is, I was working over at the radiocarbon dating lab in Seattle and staying with Jean Grover . . ." Ah ha! He'd always suspected some kind of unnatural relationship there! "And since I had a day to spare she asked me to check out the site. Before the *Geographic* crew arrives, y'see."

Like meringue in the rain, the sugary smirk on Tuliver's face crumbled.

"She's interested in emphasizing the goddess component," continued bd, savoring the moment. "Thinks that the readership'll like that."

At this latest revelation, Tuliver turned ghostlike and had to grab the table to prevent himself from losing his balance.

"This is a joke, isn't it?" demanded Tuliver when he had recovered from his near fall. "You're saying this to annoy. It's malicious and . . . and . . . and unprofessional," he concluded feebly.

bd shook her head gravely. "You know that's not true, Ian. Don't mean to come in and dictate to you, but Jean said to get the story straight. Before tomorrow."

"Story? What story? This is archaeology!" Tuliver threw his arms out wide as if to encompass the profusion of books, rolled maps, and other paraphernalia of science in action that filled the office. "The only *stories* here are those fairy goddess tales borne of *your* imagination." He thumped the table with a pudgy fist, causing a yellow mechanical pencil to drop to the floor and bounce directly into the waste bin—a thousand-to-one event, but one of no consequence.

Hannah put a calming hand on bd's shoulder. She could feel that her old friend was about to blow a vein as big and juicy as the one that now throbbed in Tuliver's bulgy neck.

"And you, Crisp," he barked, "had best get back to work. I'm not paying your expenses to sit around." Alasdair jumped up at the sound of his name and scuttled toward the door. "We shall speak later, young man," added Tuliver in a measured, headmasterly tone.

Hannah straightened up to let Alasdair pass and decided to use the opportunity to duck out. "I'm sure you don't need me here, so I'll leave you two to your business." She followed the young man out of the door. "Anyway, I've an errand to take care of."

Now that they were alone, bd pulled up the vacant chair so it faced Tuliver with only a box of papers on the floor between them. She sat primly, hands folded in front of her, and was about to make an opening move when she exploded into a festival of nasal dissonance.

"Tshh! Tshh! Tshh! Damned allergies." Out came the handkerchief, and the sufferer patted the underside of her nose that was feeling red and tender.

Tuliver sat unmoved and expressionless.

"Now, Ian, honey," began bd. "This is awkward for both of us. Hope that you believe me when I say I'm not here to usurp your role. Jean just wants to bring in another perspective."

"A woman's perspective, I suppose you mean." Tuliver turned, looked through the pitted screen of his office window, and continued in a flat tone. "I suppose the opinion of an experienced archaeologist who has paid his dues in the trenches no longer counts for anything."

Hannah might have pointed out that Tuliver's experience "in the trenches" was quite brief and many years before, but bd would take the high road. Or at least the middle road. She would appeal to his vanity. And lie a little.

"Not true, honey. Jean respects your work immensely. And your commitment to scholarly cooperation. She quoted your own opinions about—how does it go?—scholarly journals not being committed to 'enshrining some eternal Truth' but being open to other interpretations. Isn't that how it went?"

Tuliver pursed his lips, but showed no sign of annoyance. At the time, he felt that it was a damned stupid thing to have said in public, an offhanded piece of inanity that had been snagged by the editor of the Society for American Archeology's newsletter. But the quote had gotten him minor notoriety, and he was willing to own it.

"Yes, something like that. As you know," he continued, becoming expansive in the anticipation of expounding his own views, "I've never been of the opinion that one should restrain hypotheses simply because they have not yet received the imprimatur of the archaeological establishment. Academe should value diversity. Museums should be places of discourse, not shrines where the interpretations of the past are unchallenged through the generations."

"So you agree with authors who've started to give their books names like *An Archaeology of Early American Life*, which a few years ago would have been *The Archaeology* . . . ?"

"Of course," he insisted with a wave of the hand. "The implication here is that the author does not have the final word on the subject and the data may be interpreted differently by another. Discussion and change are the bases of science, even social science." Now, to be strictly accurate, Tuliver was willing to spout these liberal ideas and even to believe them in a general sort of way. Except, of course, when it came to his own work.

"Exactly," said bd with a broad smile. "That's just what Jean was saying to the editor of *American Archeologist*. 'Ian will put Cambridge University to shame,' she said."

"She said what?" Tuliver was puzzled, but intrigued.

"Oh, they were talking about how Cambridge was putting all their data on the World Wide Web. From their excavations at Çatalhöyük, that is. And how you were likely to do the same." Tuliver's eyebrows rose slightly, causing bd to add, "since you are into on-line publishing." Another slight exaggeration on bd's part. In truth, earlier that year, Tuliver had browbeaten a new graduate student into posting one of the professor's old publications, recycled from his doctoral dissertation, on the department's Web page in the hope that it would get his name cited by Web-crawling researchers.

Turning again to the window, Tuliver considered the implications for a few moments. Çatalhöyük was one of the best-known research excavations in the world. A spectacular eight-thousand-year-old Neolithic town site in Turkey, first worked on during the 1960s and now a joint effort of scholars from Cambridge, Berkeley, and prestigious institutions from around the world. Tuliver didn't mind being mentioned in the same sentence as that team. No objection at all. The Çatalhöyük Web site was famous for providing access to all the excavation data. While some hoard their information until publication some time in the nonspecific future, Ian Hodder, the Çatal project director, put it out there for anyone with a modem.

ÇATALHÖYÜK: A SITE WITH A SITE

‹http://www.catalhoyuk.org/english.htm›

Search

Mission Statement

Newsletters

Discussion Group

Join the Friends of Çatalhöyük

Archive Reports

This Web site is designed for those interested in the ongoing excavations at Çatalhöyük, Turkey. Its aim is to provide information about the activities of the Project and of the different aspects of the research being conducted at Çatalhöyük.

The Neolithic site of Çatalhöyük was first discovered in the late 1950s and excavated by James Mellaart between 1961 and 1965. The site rapidly became famous internationally due to the large size and dense occupation of the settlement, as well as the spectacular wall paintings and other art that was uncovered inside the houses. Since 1993 an international team of archaeologists, lead by Ian Hodder, has been carrying out new excavations and research, in order to shed more light on the people that inhabited the site. Find here the first results.

Recent additions

The 1999 winning entries of the British Airways competition are now available.

You can now search the documents on this web site.

Çatal News 6 - the annual Newsletter of the Friends of Çatalhöyük - has just been published.

The 1999 Archive Report is now available. This year it includes an Introduction and Abstracts in Turkish.

General Information

Search

Links

Further Reading

Excavation Diaries

Read the Newsletters for more information about the project

Read a summary account of the 1999 Excavations, which ran from April to September 1999.

If you are visiting Turkey this this summer, come and see the excavations: The site can be visited throughout the year, a neolithic house is on permanent display.

Take part in the Çatalhöyük Discussion Group.

ÇATALHÖYÜK is a really nifty 7,000- 8,000-year-old Neolithic town site in Turkey that is being excavated by an international team. The site is made up of many contiguous buildings, which were entered through holes in the roof. While many archaeologists jealously guard their data until they have time to publish, the ÇATALHÖYÜK Web page allows access to excavators' field notes so that everyone with an Internet connection may make use of and reinterpret the data. The Web page also contains an open discussion forum where participants are encouraged to question, laud, and disagree with the archaeologists' interpretations.

"Quite right. I was e-mailing just that to Hodder only the other day." The famous name dropped almost imperceptibly from his lips.

"Exactly," smiled bd, circling for the kill. "And that was where Jean saw the feminist connection, too."

"The goddess connection, you mean." His voice was cold and his defenses up again.

"If you want to put it that way. But remember, Hodder has a section on the Çatal Web page devoted to his discussions with the goddess movement. And they tour the site, too."

"I knew that," Tuliver said curtly. His mind was moving rapidly, assessing the relative gain to be made by embracing this fringe group and thereby aligning himself with the postmodern aristocracy versus the potential approbation of the more conservative group whose banner he habitually flew. "But just explain to me, if you'd be so good," he continued, "what Hodder has gained by engaging with these . . . these hairy-legged Wiccans?"

Although her allergies had temporarily abated, bd drew the handkerchief from her sleeve and delicately blotted her nose to the count of ten. If she could bear Tuliver's insolence for just a little longer.

"I'm sure you remember that James Mellaart, the first excavator of Çatal, found that many of its rooms were decorated with elaborate relief sculptures and paintings. He also found a lot of small figurines, many of which have female characteristics, including the famous Mother Goddess figure. He took all this evidence to mean that the Neolithic people here had a female-centered religion and that the buildings he had dug up were their shrines."

Tuliver sniffed, though not from an allergic reaction. "Which is why the Goddess Gang sees Çatal as the origin of what Gimbutus called 'Old Europe'—that mythical period of peaceful, egalitarian, matriarchal power that preceded the warlike empires of Greece and Rome. Yes, yes. We all know about that. But kindly explain what this mumbo jumbo has to do with the new interpretation of Çatal?"

"Quite simply, Mellaart was thinking like a modern Western man when he took the decorated buildings as having specialized, ritual functions. Unconsciously, he was looking to separate religious ritual—which he thought of as formal, hierarchical, and specialized as they are in Western cultures—from the domestic sphere, the home, which women have traditionally controlled. A feminist archaeologist like Hodder would start with a different postulate: that since many so-called primitive peoples see no distinction between religious ritual and day-to-day family life, during the Neolithic, the two were likely to have been inseparable. In fact, recent excavations at Çatal suggest just that. Portions of the floors of the supposed 'shrines' contain ordinary domestic refuse. Other areas seem to be clean. So the same room may have had both household and ritual functions."

"Or it may not," added Tuliver.

"And look at the figurines some people think are female deities," the visitor continued. "Where are they found? Not in burials or ritual places, but in house walls, on floors, and in a home grain storage bin. The evidence is mounting that the home—not some priest-dominated temple—was the center of Çatal families' religious life. Emphasizing women's roles, it's a feminist interpretation. And you don't have to be a follower of the goddess to see the value in it."

Tuliver placed his fingertips together in a small pyramid that he positioned under his chin and closed his eyes. Was he being contemplative or just ready for a nap, bd wondered?

"Well, that seems quite, ah . . . ," Tuliver searched for the mot juste, "plausible," he concluded cautiously. "And is, one supposes, no different from any other politically motivated archaeological interpretation."

bd wasn't sure how to take this remark, so she raised her chin questioningly.

"Surely you follow?" he asked. "Your feminist approach is like Marxist archaeology in that both are interested in constructing a scientifically corroborated past that conforms to their political goals. They point out, quite correctly, there is no such thing as 'raw data' in archaeology. The mere fact that we record some pieces of information and discard others says a lot about our orientation going into the research. Just as archaeologists don't interpret their sites in an intellectual vacuum, neither do they work in a political void. Evidence our conversation this afternoon." He fixed her with a particularly intense look that may have been equal parts thoughtful reflection and smirk, then turned to the window.

"I wonder," he continued wistfully, "what will become of the archaeologist's authority to interpret his—or her—site? If, in this post-modern world, all interpretations of archaeological discoveries are given a place at the table, why cannot just *anyone* dig and publish and be taken as seriously as the most respected professional? Is the profession of archaeologist worth anything if the opinion of some flowers-in-the-hair goddess seeker is equal to mine? When we discard the lifeline of objective science, where can we find ourselves but adrift in a sea of uncertainty?"

These questions did not seem to demand a response.

"Well, honey," said bd after a long silence. "Can't wait to see your site, though I must be out of here soon. I s'pose you'll want to start getting everything ready."

"Ready? Ready for what?" Tuliver roused himself from his wool-gathering and turned toward her.

"Why for the *Geographic* crew, of course. Didn't I mention they were coming?"

"Yes, yes. But I'm sure they won't be about their business until tomorrow. To get the best light." Tuliver sounded confident in his assumption.

bd got to her feet, shaking her head vigorously. "Oh no, hon. Quite the contrary. They want to set up lights and shoot tonight after dark. I imagine that they're going for a dramatic effect."

"Tonight?" bellowed Tuliver, leaping from his chair. "Tonight?"

bd grinned helplessly. "Sorry Ian. I'm just the messenger. Now, if you don't mind I'll take a look around and then head back to the mainland." With a shrug of the shoulders and one last dab at her nose, bd began to back out of the door. She found her way blocked by Hannah who, glancing up at an extremely agitated Tuliver, whispered something in the woman's ear and gestured toward a uniformed figure that began to walk toward the office.

"Looks like you-all have a visitor," said bd.

"Are the *Geographic* people here already?" he whined.

"Nope. It's a deputy sheriff. She's come to inspect the famous remains."

Tuliver's body jerked as if he had been jolted by an electrical shook. "Does everybody in the entire state of Washington know about this skeleton?" Then his shoulders drooped and his head fell in resignation.

bd felt something like compassion for the man and was on the verge of offering a word of sympathy when Tuliver regained control, evidenced by an adjustment of his tie, and abruptly announced, "All right. Wheel the witch in."

Her twinge of commiseration dispersed instantaneously and bd left with neither word nor glance. Taking Hannah's arm, she hustled her toward the excavations, hoping that the deputy, a stone-faced woman with tightly bunned hair, would give him hell.

Any casual spectator might have seen the two women move around the site with a quantity of sage head-shaking and lip-pursing; first to the finds tent and then over to the excavation. But only the most observant would have noticed a small package that slipped between the two and that the shorter figure tucked safely into her sleeve next to the embroidered handkerchief.

"M" IS FOR MARX
(KARL, THAT IS)

In Which Mr. Doyle's Ancestors Are Outed

Ian Tuliver turned the lock on the office trailer door and slumped down into his chair. What a day it had been. First there had been the insane bd starr woman. Then that tight-lipped witch of a sheriff who, in her sly tone, had virtually accused Tuliver himself of making off with the skeleton; it was now clear to him why cops wore those reflecting sunglasses. He would write a strongly worded note on university letterhead to her superior, that's what he would do.

The whole day had been exhausting. And there was still the arrival of the *Geographic* crew to look forward to. Tuliver cradled his head in his hands and massaged his temples to clear a nascent headache. Malicious colleagues, unappreciative superiors, overbearing sponsors, police harassment—the world certainly makes it tough for an honest scholar these days!

On instruction, Alasdair had made sure the crew left early that afternoon, as they would have to be back later to serve as human props for the photography session that evening. For much of the afternoon his chief had been entirely distracted by the sheriff. Then, he locked himself in the site office, yelling the occasional order through the window. So, by default, Alasdair was leader again, sucked back into his old role by the temporary vacuum of power and in spite of Terry's declaration that the site should be liberated and run as a cooperative.

The *Geographic* location crew—Hans Wurst the photographer, two lighting techs, and a sad-faced driver—arrived on the six o'clock ferry in a spotless SUV of such massive proportions that one might wonder how the manufacturer expected the thing to negotiate the narrow trails for which it was ostensibly designed. They used a cell phone to get directions, and by 6:30, the beast rolled onto the archaeological site while the sun was still high enough to set up the portable generator and lights.

In either a subtle homage to the late Danny Kaye or as a blatant rip-off of the same, the photographer's business card proclaimed himself "King of Photographers and Photographer of Kings." Tall and lanky with a shock of gray hair, Hans Wurst was dressed all in khaki topped-off with a multipocketed vest that bulged with the arcane paraphernalia of the photographer's craft. Like a cop at a crime scene, Hans commandeered the site, ordering lights and equipment arranged and rearranged as Alasdair, Terry, and Sandra sat on folding chairs drinking coffee and watching the unrolling of huge coils of orange electrical cord and the rigging of banks of silver-colored lights. While oversized Dave good-naturedly volunteered to install the portable generator on a large stump behind the finds tent, Tuliver had not deigned to show up for these mere preliminaries. Like the main attraction he felt himself to be, the professor intended to appear just in time for the photography itself and to leave immediately thereafter.

Tired equally of being a spectator and of Alasdair's snide comments about the slow and inefficient manner of the photographer's helpers, Terry wandered over to the truck with the intention of striking up a conversation with one of the crew. Better a few honest words with a member of the working class than to listen to Alasdair's reactionary drivel. And Sandra wasn't any better company, thought Terry grumpily. The blond bimbo was inoffensive enough, but she doubted that the girl had an original idea in her head.

The long-faced young man's job was to drive, maintain the supplies, and schlep the heavier pieces of equipment. That was done now and he had been sitting on the vehicle's massive rear bumper, swinging his legs and looking bored, when she approached him. Manuel—who vocalized his name as if describing a type of car transmission—was that most pitiful of workers, the student intern. Attracted by the romance of photography and the necessity to move out of the dorm, the UCLA junior spent his precious summer doing almost exactly the same as if he had worked for his Uncle Jaime's restaurant supply business.

"Only that would have been for pay," he said resentfully, prying a line of dirt from under his thumbnail with a sliver of wood. "Although this job's a lot of fun sometimes. You gotta have a sense of humor when you ride with Hanswurst," he added with the hint of a smile.

Terry nodded sympathetically, although she wasn't sure what to make of his last remark. She glanced down at her own chipped nails. "Yeah, it's the same in my field. The digging class is always getting exploited by the bosses. Even the archaeologists who claim to be radical are really part of the system. Marxism is just another theoretical model to them. Another way of interpreting their sites. It's not real politics."

Manuel looked up from his own excavation and gave an inquiring grunt. "What do you mean, sister? You saying archaeologists don't believe their own theories? And what does Marxism have to do with archaeology? Or real life for that matter," he added.

"Well, that's not quite what I meant." Terry screwed up her face to show she was serious. "Are you interested?" Receiving a noncommittal shrug, she went on. "The first thing you should know is that archaeologists are like the Viking raiders. Only instead of hitting villagers for their cattle and treasure, we go raiding other disciplines for theories about how society works and the forces that hold it together."

Manuel grinned, the first hint of animation his companion had noticed in him. "That'd be a wild scene: A bunch of old anthro profs sneaking over to the sociology department, grabbing what they can, and hightailing it back down to the second floor."

"Weeell it's not exactly like that, but a bunch of the theoretical models we use, like Marxism, didn't come from within anthropology and most of the influential thinkers aren't anthropologists, let alone archaeologists."

"You mean the French guys. Foucault, Bourdieu, and the rest. I never could keep them straight."

"You're not alone there. But don't worry about them. The most important thing to remember is that Karl Marx was first and foremost

THE CONTENTS OF KARL MARX'S BRAIN
(abridged version)

You mean to say that even some old prof who doesn't even know if it's Monday or Thursday is engaging in political action when he interprets his site?

Yes—according to Uncle Karl anyway.
He would say that the old geezer either recognizes the class conflicts that created his "data" or he ignores them. Either way, he's taking a position.
The idea that archaeologists should think about the POLITICAL implications of their work got a lot of people thinking that the field should have SOCIAL goals, rather than being a pastime for intellectuals. And that led to some of the approaches that we call POST-PROCESSUALIST.

a *revolutionary.*" An intensity passed over Terry's face as she spoke the word and her voice became gruff. "He recognized something was wrong with nineteenth-century Western society—that there were incredible inequities in wealth and power—and he wanted to fix it. But to fix it, he had to understand it. And that meant developing a model of the conditions that created the social structure of the time. What I'm saying is, he was only interested in history and sociology as the means to an end: revolution.

"Uncle Karl's basic idea, his greatest insight, was that the owners of the means of production have different and irreconcilable interests from the proletariat, the ordinary folks who work for them. Basically, he said the owners want to get everything they can out of their workers to create wealth. Meanwhile the workers want to maximize their own power in order to take back some of the wealth they created. And what's more, he thought this relationship was so clear that, unless the owners could confuse it in the minds of the proletariat, revolution was inevitable. According to Uncle Karl, this is the source of institutions like religion that create what he called a False Consciousness in the mind of the nonproperty-owning classes."

"Sure. I can see that," said Manuel, getting into the swing of things. "If you think you'll get your reward when you're dead, you won't pay much attention to unfair conditions on earth. I guess the trick is to convince the herd it's really true and that the way society is organized—with me on the top and the rest on the bottom—is just the way it should be. But I don't see what it has to do with archaeology or interning."

"Then listen. There's a guy called Sean who works here. He's a shovelbum—an archaeologist who makes his living by moving around from site to site. The other day I was trying to raise his political consciousness and I asked him why he thought he gets paid about $8 an hour while professors and company owners and the people he works for make a hell of a lot more and get vacation and sick days off. And Sean said that he supposed it's because they are better at the job than he is. They know more about archeology than he does. He doesn't want to be a shovelbum forever so he says he's going to grad school so he can get to be a higher-up himself. His bosses keep telling him that being a field technician isn't a long-term occupation. If you want to get anywhere you have to get some degrees after your name, they say.

"Now, Uncle Karl would say that the idea that being a shovelbum is only a temporary stopping-off point on the road to becoming a professor or a company owner is a myth that's perpetuated to . . ."

". . . to create a false consciousness and justify paying someone with a B.A. and experience $8 an hour. Yeah, I get it."

"How many jobs for professors of archaeology do you think there are in this country? A handful compared with the number of frikkin' Ph.D.s running around. And the same goes for real, permanent jobs with contract archaeology companies. Twenty-five years ago there may have been no place for a permanent class of low-level field archaeologists, but it's certainly not the case today. Since CRM came along, archaeology isn't just done in the summer vacations, so students aren't a reliable source of labor. The archaeological consultants couldn't survive without experienced, full-time fieldworkers like Sean and all the others. I've run into quite a few diggers who've been going from job to job for years. Which is all right until your back goes out or you get arthritis in the knees or carpal tunnel syndrome from typing site record forms on a laptop computer for weeks on end."

"And the same goes for a guy like me," said Manuel with enthusiasm. "Being an intern is like slave labor."

There was a roll of forced laughter from behind the truck.

"Are you going to lead us in a chorus of *The Red Flag* now, Theresa?" came Ian Tuliver's unmistakable drawl as he sauntered into view from behind the truck. "Surely you don't really believe academe is merely a pawn in some kind of Kafkaesque plot. Do we promise our students a life on easy street as a reward for their attempts at scholarship? I think not," he concluded in the tone favored by physicians of the old school for their patients and others of limited mental capacity.

"I was just making the point," said Terry through gritted teeth, "that, from a Marxist perspective, knowledge is just another commodity that's bought and sold like automobiles, oil futures, or . . ." She mentally scouted around for another example as Tuliver ambled past.

"Or ladies' hair products?" he suggested carelessly over his shoulder.

The skin at the roots of Terry's own dye job turned crimson, her work-hardened fists clenched, and if profanity could kill, it would have been all over for Ian Tuliver. Instead, he strolled off down the trail with a wave. Evidently, an important fax was waiting for him back at the dig's office. Tuliver doubted he'd bother to return. The Germanic manners of that photographer were too much to bear; and besides, the cameo shot with his Washington Venus had already been taken.

Terry's heart rate was still as rapid as a sprinter and it seemed like only a few seconds had gone by since Tuliver disappeared into the woods when the photographer himself ran up to the truck, his loaded vest thumping against his hips. Ignoring the archaeologist, he grabbed Manuel by the shoulders and dragged him to his feet.

"Now. Quickly, Manoo-al," he declared. "Herr Tulifer is left. Unload the boxes. Lay out the costumes. Quick, I say. We get the shoot done before . . . we get it done right quick and have beers, huh?" He gave Manuel an exaggerated wink, slapped him on the back, and dashed off into the gloom.

Terry slipped down from the truck's tailgate. "You know, Manuel," said she. "Your boss has such a strong accent, it almost sounded like he said *lay out the costumes*."

After a few moments of silence she stepped a little closer.

"Manuel? I said it sounded like *costumes*."

A grin slowly appeared on the young man's face.

"It's like I said, sister. You gotta have a sense of humor when you ride with Hanswurst."

★ ★ ★ ★

Hannah worked solidly all afternoon and into the evening and now had "G Is for Gender" virtually in the bag. While the dungeonlike atmosphere of her windowless room was claustrophobic to be sure, its lack of charm had its compensations in the lack of distraction it offered. It had been a joyously productive day. Hannah was completely focused on her work, entirely unaware that in the world outside, the sun was sinking below the hills and shadows were growing long. And that a form crept furtively out of the woods and was at that very moment making its way along the building to the very window of her bathroom, its glass pane still broken.

As Hannah struggled to think of a synonym for profligate, a hand reached inside and unlatched the window, pushing it ajar and slicing the intruder's skin on a jagged shard of glass. A droplet of crimson slid down the pane.

While Hannah mused on epistemology, someone hauled his body headfirst through the window and dropped to the floor with hardly a sound. The room was almost completely dark, lit only by a band of light that glowed pale under the door. With a blood-streaked hand, he gingerly pulled the door open a crack. Instantly it flew into his face, throwing him backwards. Hannah burst through the door in a flash, pinning the intruder face down on the floor. His left arm drawn up behind his back almost to the point of dislocation, the beleaguered interloper shrieked in agony.

At the sound of the invader's voice, Hannah released her grip.

"Sean. You idiot," she snapped angrily, helping her poor nephew upright. "In another moment I would have broken your arm."

"No kidding." Sean stretched his poor limb, massaging the wrist that had been so cruelly wrenched into such an unnatural angle.

"What the hell do you expect?" she demanded a little more gently. "Climbing through windows after dark. What are you up to?"

"Tuliver and that guy Bott were talking out on the porch and I didn't want to run into them so I thought . . . ," his voice trailed off pathetically and he looked up at her puppylike, nursing his injured paw.

"Do stop looking at me like that!" said Hannah briskly, but not unkindly. She took his uninjured wrist, hoisted Sean onto his feet, and led him out of the bathroom. He had never imagined that his aunt was so strong. But of course that isn't the kind of speculation in which a man of twenty-three usually engages in relation to middle-aged female relatives.

She sat in the only chair and threw Sean a pillow, motioning him to take a place on the floor at her feet. "I think I may board up that bathroom," said Hannah. "Seems to be a portal to the Twilight Zone. Well, boychik?" Hannah folded her arms on her chest and fixed Sean with the stern look of the wronged party.

At this point, your author draws a veil of discretion over the proceedings, unwilling as he is to pander to the voyeuristic inclinations of the depraved or to offend the delicate sensibilities of the impressionable. So there shall be no description of Sean's pitiful appearance, his forlorn and heartbroken sobs, and his dramatic howls against the mindless cruelty of fate. Freya and he had had a spat.

"And it's your fault, too," sniffled Sean. "Well, sort of."

"My fault?" Hannah shot back more in surprise than anger. "I've never even met the girl."

"Well it's not *exactly* your fault. She, Magnus, and me'd been talking about how the bones were stolen and he was saying how terrible it was."

"So the Children of Zeus didn't do it?" asked Hannah.

"Odin. Children of Odin. And, no they didn't. At least, that's what Magnus said. Anyway, somehow we got around to talking about who might have taken them, and we were listing all the people on the island. Including you."

"Thanks for the confidence."

"We were just making a list. So anyway, Freya started calling you Nana. And I said that your name was Hannah with an H. And Magnus asked what kind of a name that was, and I said Israeli, and that's when things started getting weird."

Hannah leaned toward her nephew and began to turn her bracelets as she did when thinking hard. "Weird? How do you mean, weird?"

"Well he kinda started cross-questioning me."

"About?"

"About our family and granddad and stuff. And Magnus asked if he was Jewish and I said that was pretty much required for a cantor. And then he started going on about how the Jews are not really descended from Abraham and how the northern Europeans are really the chosen people and it just got real strange. It was almost, like, anti-Semitic. And the worse part was that Freya didn't say a word. She just stood there. Oh, Hannah, what's it about?" he implored.

"I'm so sorry that you've had your eyes opened like this, Sean." She reached down and squeezed the shoulder of her sister's sentimental offspring. "I know you think history is pretty much just an interesting pastime, and that what people think about the past doesn't really matter too much. Just a bunch of professors playing intellectual games for their own amusement. Well, maybe some of it is. But not all. You've just found out that how we interpret the past, the stories we tell about past realities, have real effects on what we think about ourselves and other people. When most people in South Africa believed that their ancestors settled an unpopulated wilderness instead of a land inhabited by the Xhosas and the Bantus, don't you think that supported the policy of apartheid? It's the same with the Children of Odin. They've used some kind of twisted historical scholarship to convince themselves that white people are God's chosen. And, of course, that makes certain groups slightly less than human. In a much less extreme way, there's a parallel with archaeologists who interpret sites using models that emphasize the natural environment, or class and gender struggles, or whatever and really *believe* they are seeing the total reality—that one force is behind everything they see in the archaeological record."

"You can bring archaeology into just about any situation, can't you?"

"Yes," she grinned. "I'm hopelessly twisted that way. Just can't help trying to see pattern in human behavior. If you had an intellectual problem, boychik, we could work through it rationally. But intellectualizing doesn't always help. You need someone who can come up with a plan. Someone who can play Friar Laurence to your Romeo."

"Didn't Romeo and Juliet end up dead? Thanks, Hannah, but I'm not that far gone!"

★ ★ ★ ★

"Well, in my humble opinion, Dr. Tuliver should never have approved this . . . this charade," said Alasdair peevishly. His sackcloth jerkin and leggings itched, and the strip of leather he had been given for a belt kept getting loose, threatening to send his pants to the ground. It was incredible that Tuliver would have agreed to them dressing up like Neolithic peasants for that photographer. And it was shocking that a magazine like the *International Geographic* would go in for this sort of playacting.

"Well at least you don't have to wear a sheet and bow to the frikkin' goddess," replied Terry. "I feel like I'm at First Communion. And the thing's coming apart at the seams."

The four pseudo-Neolithic villagers huddled inside the finds tent in various stages of embarrassment, outrage, and amusement as Hans Wurst's crew gathered up the equipment in preparation for the second shoot of the evening, this one down at the tower.

Facing away from the group, Sandra was reengineering her bodice to get the best out of her less-than-extravagant chest. "You two are taking it all too seriously," said she. "Really. I think it's fun dressing up like . . . whatever it is we're supposed to be. Like Hans said, photographs are more interesting with people in them. I wonder if we'll get royalties? Did everyone sign a release?" At sixteen, Sandra had done a screen test for a horror-on-the-beach movie and, although she had not been called back, thought of herself as a Hollywood initiate. She was attractive, photogenic, and felt no shame in admitting that she enjoyed it.

Terry grunted. "You're wasting your time with that bodice, Sandra. They're not interested in your cleavage."

"Even if they could find it."

Terry gave a catlike hiss. "Ouch. That was mean, Alasdair. But I thought you liked them skinny. Seem to remember that Miss Ten-O'Clock-News was built like a poster girl for frikkin' anorexia."

A suitably caustic rejoinder began to form in Alasdair's mind, but he thought better of it as the silent, hulking figure of Big Dave began to stir in his seat. Of the four of them, Dave looked most authentic and seemed at ease in his rustic costume, although this may have had something to do with the nips he frequently took from a leather-covered flask. It didn't take much imagination to see him in the role of a sturdy Neolithic farmer enlisted by his chieftain to haul stones for some ancient megalithic monument, which was how he was cast in the photo session earlier that evening.

Alasdair stood up, hiked up his loose trousers, and tightened his belt. "We'd better be heading down to the tower for the next performance. Where did you put the lanterns, Dave?"

"Perhaps we'll run into the old guy with the mysterious rocks," suggested Sandra. "Sean said he has, like, a camp down there somewhere."

"No, no. He's left," said Alasdair a fraction too rapidly. "At least, that's what I heard."

Illuminated by kerosene lanterns at the front and rear, the group set out in single file along the woodland path whose right-hand fork would lead them to the tower. To their only observer, an elderly woman in a broad-brimmed hat, the costumed figures brought back memories of this place long ago. She shed a tear of remembrance and followed at a distance, needing no light to guide her feet.

"Wait up a bit, Dave," said Terry after ten minutes. "This goddamned sheet is coming apart again." For the fourth time, she turned away and adjusted the safety pins at her shoulder.

"I suppose," said Alasdair from his position in the rear, "to *some* people here, all this crap is an acceptable research strategy. Just another way to interpret the data, huh, Dave?"

"Postmodern bullshit," snapped Terry. She had no respect for her large colleague's theoretical orientation. And the way he hung around her got on her nerves—mostly—although she didn't like to see him picked on by Alasdair, who was always ready with a barbed comment.

"For once I agree with you, Terry."

"Don't break out the frikkin' champagne," said Terry over her shoulder. "Just because I don't go along with that fuzzy postmodern crud doesn't mean your brand of environmental determinism makes any sense."

From the back of the line, Alasdair let out what he hoped was an amused laugh. "For your information, Sandra, that was a typical Marxist response to the clear logic of the ecological approach. For some reason they just refuse to give hunter-foragers and simple agriculturists credit for being rational human beings."

"Huh?" said Sandra, feeling that the remark was addressed to her.

"I was referring to Optimal Foraging Theory. Perhaps you've heard of it? It's simply a way of understanding how hunter-foragers go about deciding what kinds of foods they'll use most. And of course that'll influence their settlement pattern and their social structure. To be brief . . ."

"Another unlikely concept," rumbled Dave, taking another hit from the flask.

". . . people will maximize the quantity of resources they accumulate by working out which type of food—salmon, for example—they can get with the smallest amount of effort. Think of it this way: in the summer it makes more sense to spend two days fishing and getting enough salmon to feed me for a week than it would to spend a week trying to collect seeds that might only last a couple of days. The theory predicts that people make the judgment whether or not the food value of a particular resource is worth the effort it takes to find it and get it ready to eat."

Sandra shrugged, not caring much either way. "Whatever."

"Yeah, yeah, yeah," said Terry, stopping the line again to take out a safety pin that was chafing her shoulder. "No one's saying that prehistoric people didn't have to eat. But it's a hell of a jump from there to speculating about their motivations. Rationally optimizing resources were they? Huh! All you've done, Alasdair, is to project the values of your own modern, capitalist society back into the past. According to you, everyone in prehistory has always been ruled by the desire to accumulate things. Resources, commodities, wealth, profit. You've just created a past in the image of the present. A typical strategy to naturalize the status quo. To 'prove' that capitalist attitudes are just a natural part of the human being and human history and our place in the natural environment. That's just frikkin' bull!"

Terry looked up and theatrically raised her palms to the sky as if asking for divine help in the extremity of her frustration. How could he be so dense?

"Everything's political with you people, isn't it?" retorted Alasdair. "Can't you conceive of any *other* influences on society and culture? Doesn't the natural environment have any role? In my humble opinion, the trouble with you neo-Marxists and critical theorists is that you only have one idea, one explanation that fits every situation. Whatever happened in the past, it *must* be due to power struggles between interest groups."

As the antagonists squared off, the little group had come to a complete standstill among the high bushes that lined the coastal path. Alasdair was standing calmly holding his lantern, while Terry gestured with passion that frequently caused the left shoulder strap on her ill-fitting costume to slide over her brown shoulder and Big Dave to look on appreciatively.

"Of course people have to eat," she declared. " But social change happens for *social* reasons! As soon as people organize themselves to survive in their environment—adapt if you prefer that word—they create social structure. And where you have social structure, there's hierarchy, with some groups taking more of the resource because they have the power. Politics wasn't invented by lefty academics. Its been a part of human social life since there was society."

Alasdair shook his head as if she had missed the point. "Fine. I'm not denying that. But it doesn't help us to understand social change as well as environmental models do. In the Neolithic, for example," he concluded, indicating over his shoulder back toward the site.

"What? Are you frikkin' nuts?" Terry smote her temple with the palm of her hand causing the loose strap to dive south once again. "There's a million articles on the Neolithic. What about Tilley's work in Sweden that we read last term? What's your humble opinion about that?"

Alasdair made no response. The truth was he'd skimmed the classic article and remembered next to nothing.

"As you *may* remember, Tilley was trying to explain changes in burial rituals that happened during the middle Neolithic, about four thousand to four thousand five hundred years ago, in southern Sweden. In the earlier period, what he called the Funnel Neck Beaker Tradition or TRB, burial rituals were very complex. The people would use the tombs over and over again. They'd crush lots of pottery vessels at the entrance to the tomb and mix up the bones of the people who were already buried there into piles. Burial rituals got even more complex as time went on when suddenly everything changed: In the period that Tilley called BAC—short for Battle-Axe/Corded Ware Tradition—the people stopped making the great offerings of pottery, and they started to bury just one person in each burial barrow. Basically, there was a whole lot less emphasis on ritual and the conspicuous destruction of wealth objects. Is any of this familiar?"

Alasdair ignored Terry's gibe. In truth, he'd never got past the confusing acronyms.

"Tilley saw this as reflecting a change in power relations within these groups. He started out with the premise that social inequalities are very clear to people who live in small, lineage-based societies like the folk of the Swedish Neolithic. To keep everyone towing the line, the group in charge has to legitimize its position by convincing the rest that their social structure is a part of the natural order. That it can't or shouldn't change. Tilley said the group in power used rituals associated with death and burial to support this ideology. The chambered tombs are massively impressive, scary, and are links to both the group's past and to the spirit world. So the powerful keep the secret ritual knowledge to themselves. During a burial, they destroyed wealth objects to make the event more memorable to the people who were watching. Then they'd mix up the bones to deny that there is any lasting difference in social status between members of the community—even though there obviously is!

"According to Tilley, the differences in wealth and power within the communities became so extreme that this kind of legitimization failed, the power of the lineages declined, and the communities became more egalitarian as shown by the simpler burial practices of the BAC period."

"Fine. So what's your point?"

"The point is that exploitative social structures don't just keep going by momentum. They have to be maintained by ideologies that support the powerful. So when I look at a chambered tomb, I see ideology and the process of social reproduction—the way the powerful actively use artifacts and ritual to keep people thinking their power is natural and right."

★ ★ ★ ★

"Hmm. No truck," observed Alasdair as the tower came into view. "I bet those photographers and their idiot driver got lost."

Terry chewed on her lip and pulled the sheetlike robe more tightly around her against the chill. She told Manuel not to take the supposed shortcut across the meadow below the site, but he had laughed her off. What could a girl like her know of driving trucks, he had scoffed.

Although she didn't know it, Terry's prediction had been right. Only half an hour earlier, Manuel had bounced the heavy rig down onto the meadow and straight into a patch of marshy ground. Soon it was hopelessly stuck, wheels slinging mud into the air with wild impotence and digging in deeper with every rotation.

"Ach! Screw it," Hans had bellowed. "We leave the thing here and come back tomorrow." He slammed his fist on the dashboard and instantly forgot all about the costumed archaeologists who were awaiting him a little farther down the road.

The tower was impressive in the failing light. Solidly built of local stone, it rose squarely above the surrounding brush. The stonework was cunningly laid to resemble the masonry of a medieval church or castle, with an arch above each narrow window and a crenellated parapet. Alasdair lifted the heavy, old-fashioned latch, and the door swung noiselessly open. The smell of sulfur emanated from white plastic bags of fertilizer that were stacked in a corner and under the open staircase. And something else. A sweet, sickening odor of decay. While Alasdair remained outside, cautiously holding the door open, Terry and Dave with his lantern stepped inside.

"Phew! Smells like something came in here to die," said Terry, holding her nose. "Looks like this was a kitchen and . . ." Her comments stopped in midstream and Dave felt a hand grab his sleeve. With a quick reaction he was able to stop her from falling hard.

"Whoa! That was like tripping on a banana skin."

Having set Terry back on her feet, Big Dave scouted around for the offending object that she had kicked back toward the door. He crouched and poked at it with a stick, and swallowed hard. The slimy object was covered with globs of blood and yellow masses that he recognized as fat. The floor was streaked with dried blood and pieces of animal tissue. Now the source of the putrid smell was clear. He rose, unsure whether or not to explain the discovery to his companion. She had not moved, was frozen, staring ahead at a rough table that stood across from the doorway. As Dave turned his lantern to the rear wall, he could see the reason for her horror. Cascading over the table's edge hung several feet of bloody entrails. The stink hit her nostrils, and Terry let out a shriek.

Alasdair and Sandra rushed inside to help and the great door swung closed behind them with a thump. Terry stepped tentatively toward the scene of carnage. Several small disembodied heads lay upon the table, their fur and long ears matted into bloody clumps.

"It's OK," cried Terry in relief. "It's only that frikkin' Rock Man. He's been butchering rabbits. Phew, what a stink. Let's get the hell outta here."

"Hate to tell you guys," said Big Dave, pushing at the door with enough force to move a small rhinoceros, "but there's a minor impediment to that plan. Because unless I'm wrong, Alasdair the Boy Wonder has just locked us in!"

The shock was palpable.

No one had ever heard Dave utter a sentence that long before.

"P" IS FOR POSTMODERN

In Which a Postmodern Kind of Truth Is Told

Driven upward to escape the stench of decaying rabbit, the four archaeologists mounted the open staircase. Soon, Big Dave's lantern illuminated what seemed to be a dead end but, on more thorough inspection, proved to be a trapdoor leading out to the roof. Once outside, Alasdair placed his lantern carefully on the top of the parapet as a beacon. All present huddled below the wall, which gave the only available protection from the breeze blowing the first wisps of fog inland. Under different circumstances, the roof would have been quite a picturesque spot.

"We're going to die up here, I just know it," whimpered Sandra.

Alasdair let out a snort of disdain, conveniently forgetting that his carelessness was responsible for the group's predicament. "It'd be a merciful release from that Marxist double-talk." Big Dave gave one of his threatening grunts, but Alasdair was cold and miserable and not in the mood to be cowed. "Although at least one can tell what the Marxists think. In my humble opinion, old Dave here is so quiet because postmodernists don't know *what* they think."

All eyes turned to the big man, who in his shy way, began to fiddle with the second lantern that started to sputter as the wick burned low.

Terry punched him playfully on the arm. "Come on, Dave. Give us the official Po-Mo position on the Neolithic."

"Be happy to. Except, as you well know, the whole point of postmodernism is the absence of an official position on anything."

Sandra stood up and stomped around, rubbing her arms to get warm. "Er, perhaps it's the cold but did I miss something? How can you have, like, a theoretical orientation that has no position?"

"A naive but oddly perceptive question, Sandy," sneered Alasdair whose mood seemed to be settling lower with the drop in temperature. "Well, how about it, big guy?"

"I don't want to bore you with the details," began Dave.

"Too late," said Alasdair under his breath.

"What?"

"I said it's late. Just get on with it, Dave."

The large one looked around sheepishly and took a hit from his flask. "Not sure where to start," he mumbled. "Although a good place would be to set Alasdair straight on the difference between postprocessual archaeology and postmodernism."

"So kind of you to help," said Alasdair coldly.

"I'm sure you'll find some opportunity to reciprocate." Dave stroked the day-old whiskers on his Neanderthal jaw and addressed himself to Sandra. "You remember that the New Archeologists were interested in finding out what cultural, social, or ecological processes are behind human history. Basically, they looked at culture as the way people adapt to their environment. Of course, this view hasn't gone away over time 'cause it's a useful way of looking at things. But as time went on, more and more of them felt that all this emphasis on forces and processes was leaving something out of the equation."

"Like, people?" suggested Sandra.

"Yep. They felt that archaeology had gotten so bound up in behavioral models and quantification that the people themselves had sort of faded into insignificance. According to the models that the processualists were using, people didn't seem to have much of a role in making their own futures. From what they wrote, it was all a matter of forces acting on each other. Now, obviously, people aren't free agents who create societies and cultures without regard to the actual conditions in the real world. But the new generation, called postprocessualists because they responded to the excesses of the New Archeology, insisted that history involves real people making actual decisions.

"The Marxists and that lot have been saying this for years and sort

ACADEMIC SMACKDOWN !!

THE EMPIRICAL, MODERNIST ARCHAEOLOGISTS
They don't believe nothing they can't count!

vs.

THE INCOMPREHENSIBLE, FRENCH, PO-MO PHILOSOPHERS
So obtuse that they can't even understand each other!

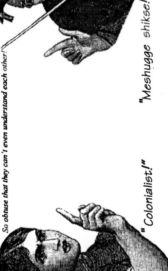

"Colonialist!"

"Meshugge shikse!"

THE MODERNISTS...

REALITY *exists. It's independent of our conceptualizations of it*

THERE *are objective facts & we can know them*

THINGS *have definite meanings*

PROOF *comes from scientific endeavor*

FIXED *canon guides research*

ACADEMIC *study*

BEHAVIOR *is patterned*

DISTANCE *from subject is desired*

ETHNOGRAPHY *is the product*

ANALYSIS *reveals structure*

THE POSTMODERNISTS...

REALITY *is a construct. It's a function of how we conceptualize it*

ALL *knowledge is relative*

THERE *are endless interpretations*

PROOF *is a fallacy, an illusion*

DIVERSE *approaches to research*

PRAXIS

BEHAVIOR *is variable*

PARTICIPATION *with subject is mandatory*

DECONSTRUCTION *is the goal*

ANALYSIS *reveals writer's presuppositions*

So two archaeologists walk into a bar.

"I published my book with a $10,000 grant from the National Science Foundation," says the first.
"Yeah, I know," says the second. "I just got $12,000 from the National Endowment for the Arts to deconstruct it."

of joined forces with other folks who used nonprocessual approaches like structuralism and feminism to create a bunch of alternatives to the orthodoxy of processual archaeology. So what it comes down to is that there are lots of approaches that could get labeled postprocessual simply 'cause they reject processualism."

"How does postmodernism fit in?" asked Sandra as Alasdair and Terry groaned in unison.

"That's a whole book in itself. But I'll tell you how it relates to one postprocessual approach that's called contextual or interpretive archaeology, although no one seems to want to saddle it with a permanent tag. People who take this approach don't like the notion that you can account for what happened in the past—or the present for that matter—by a single theory, be it economic, environmental, psychological, or whatever. In fact, they tend to think these so-called metatheories just box us in and make us think in one dimension about the things we dig up. Interpretive archaeologists say that artifacts have no fixed meaning that we can uncover. They say the meaning of an artifact to the people who used it depended on the context in which it was used."

"Like Jim Deetz's example of the candle," chipped in Sandra, pleased that she could follow Dave's train of thought. "A candle's, like, a utilitarian object when we use it to light a dark corner. Or a romantic symbol if you put a couple on the dinner table. Or a religious object during a Catholic Mass."

"Right. So we can never know what an artifact means without first knowing the context it was used in. Interpretive archaeologists say that artifacts are like texts: you can either understand literally or as metaphor. And in the same way that artifacts don't have fixed meanings, neither is there one single past out there to be known. The critical theorists and the feminists and the rest have their perspectives, but none can claim to explain it. All they can do is to interpret it."

"Now just a minute, big guy," interrupted Alasdair. "If artifacts and sites are texts that have a variety of meanings, then how can we ever know what happened in the past?"

"We can't. At least not in the way you mean it, since there was no one past to know."

"If I thought that was true I'd give up archaeology as a waste of time."

"And a thousand archy sites sigh with relief," put in Terry. "But for once and probably the last time this decade I agree with you. This contextual approach or whatever you call it is an intellectual dead end. In fact it's a step backwards."

"Quite so," interrupted Alasdair. "In my humble opinion, the whole approach is hopelessly relativistic. If there's no actual past, no facts, and no understandable meanings out there, then how do we decide what's a reasonable approach to take to understand the past? If everyone has a seat at the table, are you going to set a place for that nut Erich von Däniken who thinks extraterrestrials built the pyramids, as well as for Dr. Tuliver? And what about the Children of Odin? Just because *they* believe their imaginary gods have sent them out here to rebury the skeleton we dug up, does it mean we have to hand it over?"

Not waiting for Dave to defend himself, Terry jumped into the argument.

"Alasdair's right. Relativism is a dead end. If you say that the past is up for grabs, you totally trivialize the great themes that run through human history—like the class struggle—by giving them weight with every flaky idea from the front page of the frikkin' *National Enquirer*. I don't know if archaeology's a science or not, but I do know we have to give our research agenda some priorities or the field will disintegrate into a million particularistic studies that have no connection with each other."

Dave nodded somberly. At first, the half-pint of vodka loosened him up, but now it was starting to slow him down. "Yeah. I'm not saying you're wrong. There's some danger of that, I suppose. But think of the alternative. We don't write history with Europe at its center anymore 'cause we recognize it's ethnocentric. Well, in the same way, I can't see throwing interpretive models out of the window 'cause they're not part of the accepted intellectual tradition. I'll certainly agree that the view we end up with isn't as coherent and comforting as your cut-and-dried social science models. But it's certainly more interesting."

Wisps of fog floated by, barely visible in the gloom. Sandra shivered and warmed her hands around the lantern. The others seemed to be warming up by mere argument, but as the chill set in, she found the discussion increasingly boring and trivial, considering their predicament. She preferred the old model Dave, the silent but considerate one. He hadn't even offered her a hit from his flask. For the last few minutes, she had seriously considered trying to squeeze through one of the window slots or scaling the wall. It was a long way down, but the irregular stones would give her some foothold, she imagined. And she'd rather risk hitting the ground with a splat and getting it over with.

For anything would be better than suffering the agony of this interminable Death by Theory.

★ ★ ★ ★

"Ach! They're off having a party with Manuel and my crew, I bet," said Hans, casually taking another bread roll from the platter. "You know how the kids are." He ripped the roll in half, slathered it with enough butter to clog a minor artery, and looked around the dining room table for more.

Ian Tuliver, whose own concept of a healthy diet consisted of eating the pickle on his hamburger, regarded the photographer with a look of contempt. "But where *are* they, Mr. Wurst? You say that you arranged to meet them and they didn't show up."

"Ja. Something like that." A fair portion of a chicken leg disappeared into Hans's mouth.

"Then where *are* they?" repeated Tuliver. He looked around at Ollie Bott for support, but the excavation's patron was hidden behind a newspaper, his feet up on the couch.

Hans shrugged. "Got lost, maybe. If you so concerned, you look for them, Herr Tulifer."

"I dispatched Dr. Green to search an hour ago. She knows the area surprisingly well and it would do no good for me to go blundering about in the dark."

"Ah, sure. The Green and the old woman, they find 'em all right."

"Old woman? What old woman was that?" Bott spoke from behind his newspaper, and there was an uncharacteristic tone in his voice that might have been anxiety.

"I donno. Some old woman in the big hat. They walking together down that path toward the ocean."

"Talking?"

"Sure talking. What else would they be doing?"

The newspaper was down now, and Bott's uneasiness showed in his face.

"Mr. Bott," said Tuliver impatiently, "I fail to see that this has any relevance to the task at hand. I am personally responsible for the safety of these students and . . ."

"Keep your pants on, Tuliver. You're becoming a real pain in the be-hind."

"This is intolerable," sputtered Tuliver, jumping up from his chair. "I don't have to come here to be insulted."

"Ja?" asked Hans, shaking his mangled chicken femur at the red-faced professor. "Where you usually go then? Huh? Ha! Ha!"

Tuliver snatched up his briefcase and threw a look of scorn at Bott. He should never have gotten involved in this project. The Austrian was clearly insane and Bott was worse. The man had no conception of science and was capable of anything.

Providentially, the evidence of exactly what Hans was capable of had appeared in the doorway a few moments before and had been watching the scene unfold. The anachronisms of their pseudo-Neolithic garb that had been softened in the lantern light were exposed in the indifferent glare of the bare electric bulb. They were humiliated, hungry, cold, and angry.

"What is this? A costume party?" snapped Tuliver, looking his students up and down. "You have inconvenienced Mr. Wurst, Dr. Green, and myself by your unprofessional behavior."

Terry elbowed Alasdair in the ribs. "I told you he didn't know about the costumes. And he was the one who didn't show up." Terry tried to simultaneously hold her robe together and point at Hans. "If Dr. Green and Miss Bott hadn't rescued us we'd still be stuck up in that frikkin' tower."

The motley group swarmed into the room and dumped themselves into chairs and couches. Miss Bott, an elderly lady carrying a broad-brimmed hat and with Hannah on her arm, took a position on the couch next to Ollie. For once, he seemed speechless.

"And what are *they* doing here?" demanded Tuliver, pointing to Sean and Freya who hovered uncertainly at the door. "This is a madhouse. Costumed players trapped in towers with Druidic princesses. Whatever next?" Evidently, the lovers had bridged the ethnic divide that had briefly separated them, for they stood hand in hand.

"They're here because they have *information* that concerns you and you." Hannah nodded firmly at Tuliver and Ollie Bott in turn.

"Have you been asleep for the past week, Green?" groaned Tuliver in frustration. "That is one of the despicable group who made off with the skeleton."

"Are you sure of that?" said Hannah mysteriously. "Did you ever wonder how they got to hear of the remains when only the archaeological crew knew about them?"

All eyes turned to Freya, who tossed her hair and said quite simply, "Someone left a message on the altar where we do . . . er . . . did our afternoon ceremonies. All it said was that the archaeologists had dug up the skeleton of a European. That's all. So we went on over."

"Oh, very likely. And it was signed 'A Friend,' am I right?" scoffed Tuliver. "I blame television for the present generation's failure to distinguish reality from fiction."

"Matter of fact, it was signed 'A Friend.' And I know what I saw," countered Freya stiffly.

"Then it was that viper." Tuliver indicated Sean with the smallest inclination of his head. "He must have slunk off surreptitiously and left the note."

Terry spoke up. "Nope. He was working with me the whole time."

"Then who done it?" spluttered Tuliver.

"Did it," corrected Hannah pedantically. "Whom did you tell, Ian?"

"Only Mr. Bott here," he indicated Ollie, who had remained uncharacteristically quiet since the group's arrival. "Surely you're not suggesting that he had anything to do with it? You have completely lost your senses, Green. This does not bode well for tenure, you know."

Hannah ignored Tuliver's threatening remark and turned to Alice Bott, who was smiling angelically at nothing in particular.

"Miss Bott, you grew up here on Dougal's Island, didn't you? Do you remember how things used to be here in the old days?"

"Oh yes," said the old woman. "Occasionally I find myself forgetting things that happened yesterday, but my girlhood's as clear as crystal. Strange how that happens, isn't it, dear? I must be getting old." Miss Bott faded off into silence and was gently put back on track by Hannah.

"I was in one of the last classes here," she gestured around vaguely. "I graduated in '32 with Milly Stewart, Bettina and Marina Shannon, Victoria Fine, Violet Huff, and Dotty McInnes. There're all gone now, except for Dotty. Never did care much for Dotty. And after that, I stayed on to help Mother with the younger girls with ancient history and such. Mother was very keen on ancient history, you know. Particularly British history. Her family was from England, you know. Somewhere out in the West Country where they have all those marvelous megalithic monuments. Marvelous megalithic monuments," she said again, savoring the mellifluous sound of the phrase, and drifted off into a reverie once more.

"Miss Bott? Do you remember what you told me about the ceremonies at the mound?" asked Hannah softly.

Freya looked up with interest and gripped Sean's hand.

"Oh yes. Mother was a strong believer in the Old Religion. I think she thought of herself as a priestess," said Miss Bott confidentially. "On special nights, the equinoxes and such, all we girls would dress up in our robes and make offerings to the carving of the great goddess. Ah, the memories. When I saw those young girls today, all dressed up and looking so pretty," she smiled kindly at Terry, "it brought it all back. Milly, Bettina, and me."

"And when your mother passed away? Do you remember that?"

"Oh yes, dear. But it was such a long time ago. She wanted to be buried here on the island. I was quite young at the time, and pretty, too, though you would hardly know it now." She paused, fishing for a compliment with which Hannah obliged.

"And she was buried . . . ?"

"In the old way, just as she asked. Didn't I just tell you this, dear?"

"What do you mean, Miss Bott, 'in the old way'?"

"Oh, like the ancient women of the deep past. In her stone crypt out under her mound."

"What?" Tuliver popped out of his chair as if he had sat on a bee. "Are you claiming that the skeleton I . . . we uncovered is only sixty years old? I won't believe it! And besides, it's gone, so there's no evidence."

"Except for the bone sample that I sent off with my friend bd starr for radiocarbon dating," added Hannah. "I imagine that will clear up any ambiguity."

"But the mound itself and the carving," said Tuliver, desperately clinging to the arms of his chair. "Surely they are authentic."

"Oh yes, dear," smiled Miss Bott. "Entirely authentic."

Tuliver let out a sigh of relief and flopped back into his seat.

"Mother herself cut the picture of the Great Goddess from the *International Geographic* and had it carved by Miss Whitmore, our sculpture teacher. Miss Whitmore was a niece of Sir Henry Whitmore, who was commissioned by Prince Albert himself for a portrait. Perhaps you've heard of him?"

Stifling a laugh, Hans Wurst emitted a kind of snort.

"And the mound?" groaned Tuliver, caring nothing of Sir Henry's illustrious career.

"Accurate down to the smallest detail," smiled Miss Bott luminously. "A perfect copy of Oldgrange Barrow in the English West Country. Have you found the passage in your diggings, Professor Toliphant? I recall we had a tea party there in the spring of '24, before the laborers filled it over. It was a glorious year, you know. Happy days and moonlight picnics on the beach with Mother. All gone now," said the old lady dreamily. "Past and gone."

At this, Hans's laughter overwhelmed his ability to restrain it and he began to roar, pounding the floor with his heavy boots in mirth.

"That's a great joke. Even better than mine. The great discovery, mound, carving, body. All as phony as . . . as them rented costumes." The crew moved uncomfortably in their seats, and Sandra folded her arms across her tightly laced bodice.

But Hannah shook her head. "Not quite all. The skeleton was real enough, as was the pottery. I assume, Mr. Bott, that you took the remains of your grandmother in order to keep this game going a little longer. For I'm sure you realized that any experienced archaeologist could tell a modern skeleton from an ancient one just by looking at it, and that would put a stop to everything. But I *would* like to know about the pottery."

Ollie Bott had sat quietly to this point, exhibiting neither surprise nor anger at Hannah's accusations. Now, he cocked his head to one side and smiled at her.

"Well, well. I took you for one smart lady straight off, Doc. And so you turned out to be. Figured out my little game from end to end, you did." He made a half turn toward his aunt. "And don't you worry about your mama, Miss Alice. She's planted in a real nice place out overlooking the bay. She'd like that, she would."

Although Alice Bott smiled and nodded at the mention of her name, Hannah thought it unlikely she comprehended what had become of her mother's bones.

"And the pottery sherds? Why they were easiest of all. I just paid cash for a big ol' bag through some treasure-hunting magazine and scattered 'em around up there. Glad to hear they were real. Guess I got my money's worth."

"Which would explain why the diggers found them only on the surface and not in the mound itself," observed Hannah.

"But it was an understandable error, surely you can see that," pleaded Tuliver to the assembled company. The vision of massive humiliation flashed before his eyes. Would any of his colleagues ever take him seriously again?

Tuliver's thoughts were altogether transparent to Hannah, and she maliciously let that question hang out there for a few moments before continuing.

"OK," she continued. "So now we understand how you pulled off this prank, but not why you did it. What could your motive possibly be?"

"Prank? You call this a prank, Green?" blustered Tuliver. "It's a hoax, a disgraceful fraud. And the perpetrator shall be prosecuted to the fullest extent of the law."

Bott leaned back and put his western boots up on a chair in an effective display of nonchalance.

"Now, now. Prosecuted, Tuliver? For what? For scattering some old pieces of pottery on my land? For giving a dumb-ass professor and his crew free room and board? Guess I should have told the county coroner that we was going to rebury my own grandmother's remains on my property. I'll mention it to him at our next Rotary Club meeting."

He yawned extravagantly and leaned back farther still, hands clasped behind his neck. "It's been fun, Tuliver. But now that our friend from the *Geographic* has his pictures, it's time for you all to leave."

Tuliver's mouth dropped open and a jumble of questioning sounds emerged.

"Wha . . . wha . . . ? I mean . . . Wha . . . ?"

Ollie turned toward Hans, and they chuckled conspiratorially.

"This professor ain't so smart, I don't think," said the photographer, spinning a large finger by the side of his head in the international symbol for mental confusion. "How about the lady doctor, does she get it?"

"Oh yes, she gets it," said Hannah. For the sordid truth was now clear to her: That she and Tuliver had been manipulated for the second oldest motive of all—money. "And she also has enough German to know *Hanswurst* means a joker. This is all about notoriety, isn't it? About getting publicity for this New Magik Healthing Spa or whatever you're going to call it."

"I call it a Retreat Centre. But, y'know, Healthing Spa sounds even better. Mind if we use it?"

Ignoring this impertinent remark, Hannah continued for Tuliver's benefit. The man was arrogant, mean-spirited, and malicious, but he had been used and abused, and his fragile ego had taken quite a blow.

"This is how I see it, Ian: Here's Mr. Bott stuck out here on an island in the middle of nowhere. His only asset is a hotel-sized building and a pseudo-Neolithic site built by an eccentric relative. He knows something about the recent interest in Native American religion—possibly from an introductory anthropology class—and shrewdly puts all the elements together: he'll make Dougal's Island a destination on the New Age ritual tour circuit to compete with Sedona, Arizona, and Glastonbury in England, and the rest. He has a vision of goddess worshipers, seekers of power convergences, and a host of other pilgrims flocking in and, incidentally, staying at his hotel. Perhaps he'll put up a gift shop and sell pendants in the shape of the Dougal's Island Venus."

"Another good idea. Thanks, Doc."

"But first he needs to legitimize the site. And that's where the archaeologists come in. After all, who has more authority than a university professor? If Dr. Tuliver says it's authentic, who's going to argue? And if he could get an internationally popular magazine to publicize it for him, so much the better. Well, Mr. Bott, you've won the game. I dare say that Hans's photographs will get published somewhere, even if the *International Geographic* won't be interested any longer."

"You're right there, doctor." The photographer's accent seemed to have gone the way of his cover story. "No, the folks at the *Geographic* won't be much interested in the story of a gullible professor—there's nothing unusual in that—but there's a whole raft of other mags that'll take it. Dr. Tuliver can look for his portrait in *Oracle*, *Earthtime*, and *Power Circles*."

"Not to mention *National Investigator*," added Hannah softly but enjoying every word. "Congratulations, Ian. You're going to be a celebrity now. At the supermarket checkout stand, that is . . ."

Epilogue

In Which Everyone Gets Just What They Get

If this tale was pure fiction, your author—sensible of the effect of high literature on impressionable minds—might have considered introducing some deus ex machina to ensure that evil was punished and that the virtuous received their just rewards. (Several scenarios have, in fact, just flashed into his head.) However, for better or worse, this tale is about the practice of archaeology, which no one but the severely myopic could confuse with the so-called real world.

Thus, we are left with the kind of morally equivocal ending that will no doubt be abhorrent to television evangelists and others with little tolerance of ambiguity of any sort.

- They are the kind of people who would appreciate neither this book nor its message.
- They are the kind of people who expect science to provide all the answers and feel let down and fearful when it doesn't.
- They get from archaeology as much as they are willing to give. Expecting and accepting only hard answers phrased as facts, they ask questions that can be answered in these terms.

And that, I suppose, is OK for them.

But you, o wise and perceptive reader, can see further.

You, perhaps, have concluded, as Sean suggested in chapter 1, that archaeologists can do no more than tell stories about the past. Some are stories of harmony, others of discord. Some pass the test of Oc-cam's Razor; others don't. Some sound plausible, but have no data to back them up.

An eminent archaeologist once used the onion analogy to describe the process of doing archaeology. Archaeologists strip away the layers, he wrote, and find the truth at the center. Sounds profound, but it's misleading because—at least in the opinion of your author—it pre-supposes that there is a *truth* out there to be found. A better analogy, although without any gustatory appeal, might be one of those pic-tures made up of thousands of multicolored dots. If you look at the picture through a red lens, you see one image, with a blue lens a dif-ferent image, and so on. Theoretical models are like these colored lenses, for they help us see patterns in the archaeological record that would otherwise be invisible. Different lenses are useful for seeing the various elements of the image. None shows all of them, and it is up to the observer to decide which image is the most revealing for his or her purpose.

The archaeological record contains many levels of meaning. On the surface level, we can discover the dates and designs of things, of who did what and where. That much is easy and needs only tech-niques, not theories. But to dig below the surface (so to speak), to speculate about *why* people did what they did—either consciously or as unknowing participants in a never-ending historical/political/eco-logical process—*that* requires a tolerance for ambiguity. It also helps to have some humility, to recognize that today's stunning insights may tomorrow be no more than orange peels on the compost pile of in-tellectual history.

★ ★ ★ ★

Returning to this manuscript after a hiatus, your author feels it his duty to bring the long-suffering reader up-to-date on the fates of our characters.

IAN TULIVER, Ph.D., RPA, F.R.S.A., received a complimentary write-up in *Power Circles* magazine and has recently accepted the position of Dean of the School of Psychic Archaeology at the University of Invercargill, New Zealand. He serves as editor-in-chief of the *Journal of Really Neat Old Stuff*.

Dr. Tuliver accepts the deanship.

Another hard day at the office for Hannah.

HANNAH GREEN is currently interim Director of Antiquities for the new Palestinian State. An enthusiastic sportswoman—she placed eighteenth in a recent Jerusalem Marathon—Hannah also enjoys whitewater rafting on the river Jordan, and is an occasional contributor to *International Geographic*.

SEAN DOYLE is Assistant Manager of the New Magik Healthing Spa and Retreat Centre. **FREYA** and he are raising their twins in the mainstream Wiccan tradition.

And they lived happily ever after. Mostly.

FINIS

For Further Reading

For anyone who might still be reading (as well as those who just skipped to the end), I offer the following books, articles, and Web sites for your edification. Please note that these references are not intended to provide a true introduction to the various subjects. Rather, I provide references for the studies mentioned in the text as well as some of my personal favorites. For a highly readable introductory survey of archaeological theory by one of the sharpest thinkers around, I strongly recommend Matthew Johnson's aptly titled *Archaeological Theory: An Introduction* (Oxford: Blackwell, 1999). If you are cyber-addicted, the U.S.-based Web site *ArchNet* and its European equivalent *ARGE* are the best sources for things archaeological. Find them at <http://archnet.uconn.edu/> and <http://odur.let.rug.nl/arge/tindex.htm> [both accessed 7 August 2000].

Chapter 1. Science and Politics in Archaeology

Professional conferences are great places to observe the behavior of archaeologists in their natural habitat. Registration fees can be high, although students usually get a reduced rate; I would *never* suggest that anyone try to sneak in without paying. Many societies' Web sites are listed at <http://archnet.uconn.edu/topical/societies>. For conferences in Britain go to <http://www.britarch.ac.uk/briefing/confs.html> [accessed 7 August 2000]. Whether archaeology is a science or not, it certainly can be practiced as a rigorous *social* science. This book's a bit dated and can be heavy going, but it's a classic statement all the same: *Archeological Explanation: The Scientific Method in Archeology*, by Patty Jo Watson, Steven LeBlanc, and Charles Redman (New York: Columbia University Press, 1984). For those interested in methodological rigor in cultural anthropology, delve into *Research Methods in Anthropology: Qualitative and Quantitative Approaches*, by Harvey Bernard (Walnut Creek, Calif.: AltaMira Press, 1995). It is one of those rare books that is both scholarly and very readable, and it includes a table of random numbers for the truly committed. Science is all very well, but archaeology has real life-and-death implications in places like Cyprus, Israel, and the former Yugoslavia. For an excellent and very readable account, try *Between Past and Present: Archaeology, Ideology, and Nationalism in the Modern Middle East*, by Neil Asher Silberman (London: Anchor, 1989).

Chapter 2. CRM, Ethics, and Pseudoscience

To find a place on an archaeological excavation in North America and, to a limited degree, in other parts of the world, go to the Archaeological Fieldwork Server at <http://www.sscnet.ucla.edu/ioa/afs/testpit.html> [accessed 7 August 2000]; for projects in Britain try <http://www.britarch.ac.uk/briefing/field.html> [accessed 7 August 2000]. Thinking of going into the lucrative field of archaeological consulting? First, read this short novel or another in the series: *Burial Ground: An Alan Graham Mystery*, by Malcolm Shuman (New York: Avon, 1998). The author gives a very realistic depiction of the life of a contract archaeologist (except for all the murders, that is), and it's a good read, too. For another kind of fantasy, the Sandia Cave controversy is presented in journalistic style in D. Preston's article, "The Mystery of Sandia Cave," *The New Yorker* (12 June 1995): 66–83. In case you're wondering if archaeologists really do have ethics, read about them in *Archaeological Ethics*, edited by

Karen Vitelli (Walnut Creek, Calif.: AltaMira Press, 1996). For an enjoyable tour of forgeries, naive misinterpretations, and pseudo-science, I recommend *Frauds, Myths, and Mysteries: Science and Pseudoscience in Archaeology,* by Kenneth Feder (New York: Mayfield Press, 1997).

Chapter 3. The New Archeology and Its Predecessors

The best survey of archaeological ideas is *A History of Archaeological Thought,* by Bruce Trigger (Cambridge: Cambridge University Press, 1989). For an original and controversial view of history and archaeology from the 1930s, see if you can find a copy of *Man Makes Himself,* by V. Gordon Childe (London: Watts Publishing, 1936). For those who just can't get enough of the New Archeology, try *A Study in Archaeology,* by Walter Taylor (American Anthropological Association, Memoir No. 69, 1948). The statement that may have ushered in the New Archeology is "Archaeology as Anthropology," Lewis Binford, *American Antiquity* 28 (1962): 217–25. It's also a premier example of the kind of jargon-riddled writing that still plagues our field. For a stunning view of what some New Archeologists achieved, take a stroll through *The Early Mesoamerican Village,* edited by Kent Flannery (New York: Academic Press, 1976).

Chapter 4. Ethnoarchaeology and Cultural Ecology

The story of Lew and Eskimos can be read in greater detail in Lewis Binford's *Nunamiut Ethnoarchaeology* (New York: Academic Press, 1982). A very different approach to ethnoarchaeology is taken in *Symbols in Action,* by Ian Hodder (Cambridge: Cambridge University Press, 1982). To see how a British archaeologist began to tease out the complex relationship between culture and environment, try *Excavations at Starr Carr,* by Grahame Clark (Cambridge: Cambridge University Press, 1954). A version of this classic case study is frequently reprinted as an educational module by Addison-Wesley Publications.

Chapter 5. Diffusion and Classifying Societies

My discussion of bands, chiefdoms, and the rest comes from *Primitive Social Organization,* by Elman Service (New York: Random House, 1971). Although the author presents his scheme as social *evolution,* I prefer to think of it as a purely descriptive model. Diffusion of ideas is a fact (there, I said the word), but in itself doesn't really explain much—as the New Archeologists insisted—and can be deceptive. An example of the extreme (and extremely unscholarly) use of diffusion as explanation is *Bronze Age America,* by Barry Fell (Boston: Little, Brown, 1982). It's a good laugh, but don't take it seriously.

Chapter 6. Cannibalism and the Native Peoples/Archaeology Relationship

Was cannibalism largely the invention of nineteenth-century Europeans who wanted to rationalize their imperialist tendencies? This position is taken by W. Arens in *The Man-Eating Myth* (New York: Oxford University Press, 1979). A very different view of the controversy comes from that other institution (Cambridge) in *Divine Hunger,* by Peggy Sanday (Cambridge: Cambridge University Press, 1986). If you read only one book on cannibalism this year, make it the latter. Archaeology's love/hate relationship with Native Americans is exposed in *Skull Wars: Archaeology and the Search for Native American Identity,* by David Hurst Thomas (New York: Basic, 2000). Thomas, an internationally respected scholar with an excellent writing style, puts the Kennewick Man controversy in historical context.

Chapter 7. Gender

For a review of the issues and professional literature, try *Gender in Archaeology,* by Sarah Nelson (Walnut Creek, Calif.: AltaMira Press, 1997). My discussion of Aztec women's work comes from Elizabeth Brumfiel's "Weaving and Cooking," in *Engendering Archaeology,* edited by Joan Gero and Margaret Conkey (Oxford: Blackwell, 1991),

224–51. To learn how women's roles changed among the Inca, I recommend "Gender, Space, and Food in Prehistory," by Christina Hastorf, in *Engendering Archaeology*, 132–59. Those fascinated by the
concept of a third gender and the method of ethnohistory should
read Sandra Holliman's "The Third Gender in Native California," in
Women in Prehistory, edited by Cheryl Claassen and Rosemary Joyce
(Philadelphia: University of Pennsylvania Press, 1997), 173–88.

Chapter 8. Marxist-Influenced Archaeology

To learn more about how the chieftains of Neolithic Sweden may
have used material culture to maintain their power, try this rather
complex chapter by Christopher Tilley: "Ideology and the Legitima-
tion of Power in the Middle Neolithic of Southern Sweden," in *Ideology, Power, and Prehistory*, edited by Daniel Miller and Christopher
Tilley (Cambridge: Cambridge University Press, 1984), 111–46. If
you're interested in seeing where other archaeologists have taken the
ideas of Uncle Karl, I recommend *The Archaeology of Inequality*, edited
by Randall McGuire and Robert Paynter (Oxford: Blackwell, 1991).
The editors' introductory essay is particularly good.

Chapter 9. Postprocessual Archaeologies

Here are a couple of books that give a feel for the subject, though I'm
not sure that my first author would approve of being put in this cate-
gory. Somewhere, I have to mention a very influential book that is
cited by scholars and is fun to read (inexpensive, too): *In Small Things
Forgotten: An Archaeology of Early American Life*, by James Deetz (New
York: Anchor Books, 1996). A thoroughly postprocessual, "reflexive"
approach to archaeology is offered in *The Archaeological Process*, by Ian
Hodder (Oxford: Blackwell, 1999). Hodder's final chapter, "Towards
Nondichotomous Thinking in Archaeology," presents a radical new
approach that redefines archaeological evidence and challenges old
notions about who has the right to interpret it. Excellent stuff.

Talking Points

Use the theoretical discussions engaged in by our protagonists as jumping-off points, places to begin on the journey of teasing out meaning and separating mere opinion from reasoned conclusions. Remember, it's more important to start out in archaeology by getting an understanding of its *logic* than by memorizing who invaded whom and which culture's pots have that squiggly line around the top. At least, that's my reasoned conclusion.

Some folks who don't have much of a background in archaeology may have to do some research before they can deal with these questions. So get to it.

Chapter 1

What is science? Are the social sciences so different in method from the hard sciences like chemistry? Who decides which research questions are *worth* pursuing? What did Hannah mean when she said that she liked to think of herself using "the methods of science to approach questions that are humanistic?"

Chapter 2

What is Cultural Resources Management and how different is it from archaeology? Is Occam's Razor a useful principle? What are its limits? Is it wrong for scientists to falsify their results? Why? Thinking of Claude's rocks, is there a point where one should draw the line at open-mindedness, or is everything just a "matter of opinion"? Do you, like Sean, believe in love at first sight? (Be honest now.) Is *that* a matter of opinion?

Chapter 3

Why were the archaeologists of the early twentieth century primarily interested in reconstructing history? What's meant by a *historical* explanation of events?

Chapter 4

The New Archeologists used to say that "archeology is anthropology or it is nothing." What did they mean by that? Histories of archaeology make a big deal about the rise of the New Archeology. Was it really *that* important? Can one really make valid, species-wide generalizations about human behavior? Assuming that you could, why would you *want* to do such a thing? What do you think about the idea that culture is the way that societies adapt to their various environments? Which aspects of modern Western culture does this concept explain?

Chapter 5

How does the process of diffusion work? Can you think of any contemporary examples? (And "no" is not an acceptable response, thank you.) What's the connection between a community's social structure and its ability to create massive pieces of architecture? Put another way, could a band society have built the Egyptian pyramids? What happens to egalitarianism as societies get bigger? State societies are bigger, more rationally organized, and create far more technologically complex stuff (like computers) than bands or chiefdoms. Does that mean that state societies are *better* than bands? Is "better" a useful concept here?

Chapter 6

What are the limits of cultural relativity? Why would a scientist want to make up categories for things when cultures have their own groupings already? What's the difference between a materialist and a culturalist explanation? Which is correct? (OK, that was a trick question.) Terry insisted that no one should have the right to restrict scholars' access to information about the past. Do you agree? Sometimes, the government forcibly takes private land for some overriding public benefit; is there a point where private property rights end and the national interest in documenting the past begins? Should Native Americans and other First Nation peoples get to decide what happens to the remains of people they consider to be their ancestors? What if that means that scientists never find out how our species evolved and settled the earth?

Chapter 7

Is there *really* much of a difference between sex and gender? Is feminist archaeology politics, science, or something else? Do feminist archaeologists have to be women? Could archaeological interpretations affect contemporary attitudes toward gender roles?

Chapter 8

Archaeologists come up with research questions for their sites that they think will shed light on the *big* issues, like the processes that held societies together and those that pulled them apart. That's why there's so much interest in Karl Marx's model of history. Why was Marx so keen on revolution? What's the connection between Marx's kind of materialism and that of the functionalists? If optimal foraging theory helps us understand how people use their natural environment, why would a Marxist-influenced archaeologist object to the approach? Why are Marxist-influenced archaeologists interested in ideology?

Chapter 9

How are Marxist and feminist archaeologies "postprocessual"? Come to think of it, what is *processual* archaeology? Why do archaeologists insist that artifacts have no fixed meanings? If this is true, how are we to interpret archaeological sites? (You may want to defer the answer to that one until later . . . much later.) To what degree is there a *real*, objective past out there for archaeologists to discover?

Glossary

ANTHROPOLOGY   The holistic study of humankind from biological, social, and cultural perspectives.

ARCHAEOLOGICAL RECORD, THE   Artifacts, layers of soil, structural remains, and everything else that one finds on an archaeological site, which put together, enables us to reconstruct past human behavior.

ARCHAEOLOGY   (1) The study of past human behavior based on material remains, (2) "The most fun you can have with your pants on" (Kent Flannery). (*See* New Archeology)

ARTIFACT   Anything made or modified by people: this book, a 100,000-year-old spear point, and my former 1968 VW van.

AZTEC   The last of a series of Central American civilizations that flourished until the Spanish invasion of 1519. For five hundred years, the Aztec people created cities with massive civil and religious buildings, developed intensive agriculture, and controlled an extensive empire. (*See* State)

BAND   Term used by anthropologists to denote small societies of mobile, egalitarian, hunter-gatherer peoples. Bands are the simplest known societies. (*See* Service, Elman)

BINFORD, LEWIS   A founding father of the *New Archeology* movement. His 1962 article "Archeology as Anthropology" (*American Antiquity* 28: 217–25) inspired a generation of archaeologists, mostly in North America, to strive for greater methodological rigor and to commit themselves to the creation of an anthropology of the past. One of the great ones.

BOYCHIK   Affectionate Yiddish term for a young man.

ÇATALHÖYÜK   An eight-thousand-year-old Neolithic town in central Anatolia, Turkey.

CHIEFDOM   Term used by anthropologists to denote societies that are organized on the basis of rank—that is, people are born into their place in society. Chiefdoms are generally governed by a hereditary ruler. In contrast to *bands*, they are far from egalitarian. (*See* Service, Elman).

CHILDE, VERE GORDON   Australian-born archaeologist known for interpretations of European and Near Eastern prehistory that emphasized the role of class conflict in the creation of history. If that sounds like the philosophy of Karl Marx, you're right. His 1936 book, *Man Makes Himself,* is well worth reading.

CRM   Cultural Resources Management. The practice of protecting and managing archaeological sites and other important cultural properties through public policy and a conservation ethic.

CULTURAL DIFFUSION   The observation that ideas, technologies, and artifacts can move from one place to another, from one culture to another.

CULTURAL ECOLOGY   The study of human culture as a mechanism by which societies adapt to their varied natural environments.

CULTURAL RELATIVITY   The position that no culture is intrinsically "better" than any other. Modern British society, for example, is not superior to that of Australian Aborigines; it's just different. This idea developed in response to ethnocentric Victorian scientists who liked to rank the world's cultures, invariably putting themselves on the top of a heap of dark-skinned others.

CULTURE PROCESS   The underlying "why" of culture. Cultural process was the watchword, the Holy Grail, for practitioners of the *New Archeology* who were interested in the relationship between the social, environmental, and economic forces that drive society.

DETERMINISM   The notion that specific, identifiable factors "determine" the direction of culture and history. Environmental determinism, for example, holds that culture is largely an outcome of humans' adaptations to their natural environment: thus, environment "determines" culture.

DIGBUM   (*See* Shovelbum)

EMIC/ETIC   Categories that are used by participants in a culture versus those imposed by the scientific observer.

EMPIRICIST   One who believes only what can be directly observed.

EPISTEMOLOGY   The study of how we know what we think we know.

ETHNOARCHAEOLOGY   The study of the cultural practices of contemporary peoples for clues by which to understand the archaeological record.

FEMINIST ARCHAEOLOGY   An approach that places women at the center of archaeological analysis to restore gender balance to the history of "man." (After Joan Gero.)

FUNCTIONALISM   A theoretical approach that emphasizes the adaptive function of cultural traits. Functionalism sees an analogy between the elements of a given culture and the organs of a living creature. In both cases, it is claimed, the parts work together to ensure the survival of the whole.

GENDER   Social categories, such as "gentleman" and "lady," that are full of cultural expectations of the people we put in them. A person's role in society has more to do with his or her socially defined gender than with biological sex.

GIMBUTAS, MARIJA   Archaeologist and art historian who proposed that Neolithic societies in southeastern Europe were peaceful, matrifocal, and goddess-worshiping. Although her 1982 book *The Goddess and Gods of Old Europe* does not have much support among archaeologists, Gimbutas's work is heavily cited by followers of the Goddess movement.

GRIMES GRAVES   Deep, extensive Neolithic-era flint mine in central England.

HODDER, IAN   British archaeologist, the excavator of *Çatalhöyük*, known as one of the chief proponents of a *postmodern* archaeology. His 1999 book, *The Archaeological Process,* isn't light reading, but it's well worth the effort.

HUNTER-GATHERER/FORAGER   Peoples who make their living by . . . ah . . . hunting and gathering. Hunter-gatherers live in simple *band* societies now and back into the *Paleolithic.*

INDIGENISM   The assumption that a group's culture developed by its own independent invention, rather than by contact with other peoples.

KENNEWICK MAN   A nine-thousand-year-old skeleton found near Kennewick, Washington. While local Native Americans claimed the remains as an ancestor and wished to rebury them, a group of scientists filed suit to study what they believed was a unique archaeological discovery that could add to our knowledge of the peopling of North America. A matter of "your data is my grandmother."

KENYON, KATHLEEN   A pioneer of stratigraphic archaeological excavation in the Near East, notably at Jericho, during the 1950s.

MAMSER   Yiddish for bastard. An insult in any language.

MARX, KARL   Do I really have to explain this one? OK, then. Nineteenth-century German philosopher, historian, sociologist, and revolutionary. Came up with the idea that human history is driven by conflict between social classes. (*See* Materialism)

MATERIALISM   The idea that the material conditions of life determine how we see the world, rather than the reverse.

MIDWESTERN TAXONOMIC SYSTEM   In 1939, the system took a stack of local cultural chronologies and turned them into a single, coherent synthesis that described the development of Native American cultures in the American Midwest.

MIDDLE RANGE THEORY   Ideas that help us link the things that we dig up with the processes that created them. (*See* Ethnoarchaeology)

MOHENJO-DARO   A fabulous archaeological site on the Indus River in Pakistan that was abandoned about four thousand years ago. The city, whose population would have been about twenty thousand, is famous for its strict grid plan and very sophisticated drainage and refuse disposal systems. (*See* State)

NATIONAL HISTORIC PRESERVATION ACT   A U.S. law that requires, among other things, that federal agencies "take into account" the effect of their activities on important archaeological sites and other cultural resources. Sometimes referred to by cynics as the Archaeologists Full Employment Act. (*See* CRM)

NEOLITHIC   A period of Old World prehistory characterized by the development of agriculture, which in turn led to the establishment of permanent settlements and complex societies.

NEW ARCHEOLOGY   A movement involving mostly North American archaeologists that emphasized using the *scientific method* and quantification to study cultural processes rather than "mere" chronology. I have intentionally left out the second "a" in the word archeology in keeping with the practice of the New Archeologists, who saw it as archaic and a symbol of European hegemony. (*See* Processual Archaeology and Binford, Lewis)

OCCAM'S RAZOR   A logical principle: the simplest explanation is the most likely to be true.

PALEOLITHIC   The period of prehistory that extends from the earliest traces of human culture 2.5 million years ago to about 10,000 years before the present.

POSTE RESTANTE   A place to pick up your mail when you have no permanent address.

POSTMODERNISM   A philosophy that rejects the traditional structure of scientific investigation and scientific authority itself.

POSTPROCESSUALISM   A critical reaction to the functionalism of the *New Archeology* that insists that people have a role in creating their own history and culture. Postprocessual approaches include feminist, neo-Marxist, and contextual archaeologies. (*See* Processual Archaeology)

PROCESSUAL ARCHAEOLOGY   The approach favored by practitioners of the *New Archeology*. (See Culture Process; Materialism; New Archeology; and Scientific Method)

PROVENIENCE   The exact place where an artifact is found.

PURPLE HAZE   Rock music piece written by Jimi Hendrix and recorded by him in 1967.

RADIOCARBON DATING   Devised in 1949, radiocarbon dating enabled archaeologists to work out the exact age of artifacts made of wood, bone, and other organic materials. It revolutionized archaeology.

RESEARCH DESIGN   A plan that lays out the investigator's theoretical scheme, research goals, and strategy for getting the project done.

SANDIA CAVE   Prehistoric site in the American Southwest that some suggest was planted with fake artifacts. Your author takes no position on the controversy, fearing the legal implications. However, the next time you are visiting the dentist you may care to peruse Douglas Preston's article on the subject published in *The New Yorker* (12 June 1995).

SCIENTIFIC METHOD   A way of answering research questions by systematically testing hypotheses using carefully selected data.

SEGMENTARY SOCIETY   Term used by anthropologists to denote a basically egalitarian social group ordered by kinship. Their settlements are permanent, and their economics are based on herding or small-scale agriculture. (*See* Service, Elman)

SERVICE, ELMAN   American anthropologist who devised a system to classify societies based on their complexity. (*See* Band; Segmentary Society; Chiefdom; State)

SHOFAR   Hebrew. A ram's-horn trumpet blown only at ritually prescribed times.

SHOVELBUM aka **DIGBUM**   An itinerant archaeologist who makes his or her living by moving from one archaeological job site to the next. Not such a romantic an existence as it sounds.

STATE   Term used by anthropologists to denote a highly complex, populous society administered by a tax-supported bureaucracy, police force, and justice system. (*See* Service, Elman)

TAYLOR, WALTER   Author of the 1948 classic *A Study of Archeology*, which expressed frustration with the descriptive archaeology of the era and called for the field's reinvention as an integrated study of past cultural adaptations. (*See* New Archeology)

THREE AGES [STONE, BRONZE, IRON]   A nineteenth-century system that classified ancient societies in supposed evolutionary sequence by means of their technologies. An interesting but flawed model of the way society works.

TIKAL   City in the lowlands of Guatemala built by the Maya civilization about twenty-four hundred years ago. Famous for the rich tombs of its elite ruling class and enormous temple pyramids. (*See* State)

VON DÄNIKEN, ERICH   Author of *Chariots of the Gods*, a 1971 book that suggests that extraterrestrials helped early civilizations build monumental architecture such as the Central American stepped pyramids. (*See* Wurst, Hans)

WURST, HANS   The clown or trickster character in German-Yiddish folktales. Literally, "Hans Sausage."

Index

About the Author/Illustrator

Adrian Praetzellis's first archaeological fieldwork was on the famous site at Mucking in southern England, where he spent July of 1969 schlepping wheelbarrows full of gravel in the rain. Eschewing the trades of bricklayer's laborer and assembly line worker, Praetzellis devoted the early 1970s to learning the field archaeologist's craft by digging Roman and medieval sites on the British archaeological "circuit." In 1975, tired of living in tents and derelict buildings, he and his wife, Mary, decided to seek their fortune in California. Since the late 1970s, Praetzellis has specialized in urban historical archaeology, focusing on ethnicity and social boundary maintenance as viewed through the archaeology and history of the Overseas Chinese as well as cultural change among Jews and other European immigrant groups in the American West.

Adrian Praetzellis holds a Ph.D. in anthropology from the University of California, Berkeley. He is associate professor of anthropology at Sonoma State University, where he has taught archaeology and cultural resources management since 1992 while also serving as director of the Anthropological Studies Center, a university research institute.

Breinigsville, PA USA
19 February 2010
232794BV00002B/1/P

9 780742 503595